WHAT YOUR COLLEAGUES ARE SAYING . . .

When you read Radical Excellence, *you immediately see how to aim and plan for a quality educational system. Anderson Foley's experience is powerful, and her expertise in special education is second to none. Too many educators and school leaders are caught up in the hamster wheel of a process designed to meet the needs of a few students. Kate Anderson Foley has built a resource that truly leads to school improvement happen. A must read for all who claim to be passionate about education.*

—**Barbara J. Smith, PhD**
ZPD School and Curriculum Design

In this immensely practical book, Dr. Kate Anderson Foley provides a blueprint for equity at the classroom, school, and district levels. The appendices provide specific tools that can be used to conduct and equity audit and, more importantly, to take specific steps to address inequities. Anderson Foley makes the starling claim that when schools get equity right, it helps not only special education students, but all students in the system. Therefore, this book is not just for those with responsibility for special education, but for all teachers and leaders who have a commitment to equity. With compelling evidence and insights from her roles in state and district leadership, the author takes equity out of the realm of rhetoric into the domain of fact-based leadership and practice.

—**Douglas Reeves**
Author, *Fearless Schools*

RADICALLY EXCELLENT SCHOOL IMPROVEMENT

To the leaders and educators who courageously pursue improving outcomes for every student.

RADICALLY EXCELLENT SCHOOL IMPROVEMENT

Keeping Students at the Center of It All

KATE ANDERSON FOLEY

For information:

Corwin
A Sage Company
2455 Teller Road
Thousand Oaks, California 91320
(800) 233-9936
www.corwin.com

Sage Publications Ltd.
1 Oliver's Yard
55 City Road
London EC1Y 1SP
United Kingdom

Sage Publications India Pvt. Ltd.
Unit No 323-333, Third Floor, F-Block
International Trade Tower Nehru Place
New Delhi 110 019
India

Sage Publications Asia-Pacific Pte. Ltd.
18 Cross Street #10-10/11/12
China Square Central
Singapore 048423

Printed in the United States of America

Paperback ISBN 978-1-0719-4653-4

This book is printed on acid-free paper.

Vice President and Editorial Director:
    Monica Eckman
Publisher: Jessica Allan
Senior Content Development Editor: Mia
    Rodriguez
Content Development Manager:
    Lucas Schleicher
Senior Editorial Assistant: Natalie Delpino
Production Editor: Vijayakumar
Copy Editor: Diane DiMura
Typesetter: TNQ Tech Pvt. Ltd.
Proofreader: Girish Sharma
Indexer: TNQ Tech Pvt. Ltd.
Cover Designer: Candice Harman
Marketing Manager: Olivia Bartlett

SUSTAINABLE FORESTRY INITIATIVE Certified Sourcing www.sfiprogram.org SFI-01028

24 25 26 27 28 10 9 8 7 6 5 4 3 2 1

CONTENTS

Note From the Publisher: The author has provided web content in this book that is available to you through a QR (quick response) code. To read a QR code, you must have a smartphone or tablet with a camera. We recommend that you download a QR code reader app that is made specifically for your phone or tablet brand.

ABOUT THE AUTHOR

Kate Anderson Foley PhD is a transformational leader with significant experience leading public school districts and states toward equitable and integrated services for all learners. Her work is grounded in social justice and breaking down the barriers for children who have historically been marginalized. She leads organizational change utilizing a strategic framework that ensures guaranteed and rigorous learning leading to college and career readiness for all students. Kate began her career as a special education teacher pioneering inclusive practices for students at risk and those with disabilities. Her work focused on creating conditions that fostered high expectations of adults for students and innovation which led to equitable opportunities for all learners. Kate's deep commitment to creating nimble and responsive systems that supported the whole child led her into administration, where she advocated for local, state, and federal reform. That experience led to improved academic and socioemotional outcomes for students, fair school funding, innovative health-care models, and efficient operations. As the founder and CEO of The Education Policy & Practice Group, Kate partners with local, state, and national organizations, education agencies, and various industries providing her expertise with the improvement process, professional learning communities, strategic planning, asset-based education policies, practices, special education, and consulting. Kate teaches a graduate-level special education law course to aspiring principals and superintendents through the lens of equity and the higher standard. Kate works closely with senior leadership across various sectors providing executive coaching aimed at creating growth-minded organizational cultures. Kate is the author of numerous articles and books. Her latest contribution is the book *Fearless Coaching* (2023).

ACKNOWLEDGMENTS

Experiences inform who we become. Those experiences fill our invisible backpacks and set our trajectory of this life. But that same trajectory can be disrupted so a positive one can be imagined. So it was for me. The good, bad, and the not so pretty experiences awakened me to what would be my life's work. I will continue to stand up and speak out on behalf of all children, and especially those who are farthest away from opportunity.

I want to acknowledge the enduring love and support of my family. They believe my pursuit of ensuring every child has the best education is worthy. Michael, Colleen, and Delaney, you fill me up so I can keep advocating for what's right. Thank you!

Writers write because they have something to say. Thank you Nan for always providing such a warm and welcoming place for me to be creative.

I want to acknowledge the woman-owned business collective who have helped to elevate my work around the world. Tina Anderson of Creative Juices Marketing & Events (https://www.creativejuicesny.com/), Kristen Johnson Design (https://www.kristenjohnson.co/), Jordana Halpern Communications (https://www.jordanahalpern.com/), and Casi Hall Creative (https://casihallcreative.com/). Casi took my rudimentary artwork and made it spectacular. Casi is graphic designer, photographer, and fine artist from Buffalo, New York. She focuses her work on helping women and small business owners develop their visual brand.

PUBLISHER'S ACKNOWLEDGMENTS

Corwin gratefully acknowledges the contributions of the following reviewers:

Jayne Ellspermann
Educational Leadership Consultant and Founder and CEO Jayne Ellspermann, LLC
Ocala, FL

Emmanuel Fairley-Pittman
Inclusive Education Coach
Boston, MA

Jerry Jailall
Education Consultant
Georgetown Guyana

Ron Wahlen
Director of Digital Teaching and Learning
Durham, NC

INTRODUCTION

I believe that the most important single thing,
beyond discipline and creativity,
is daring to dare.

~ Maya Angelou

RADICAL EXCELLENCE

What does "daring to dare" look and sound like for district and school leaders? What student-centered discussions at the district, school, and the classroom levels are taking place? What sources of evidence are being analyzed to determine if students are learning what it is they are meant to learn? What shifts are being implemented to respond to the academic, social, and health impacts of the pandemic? These are the topics that will be explored, along with practical resources that, when comprehensively implemented, can lead to a radically excellent school improvement process and improved outcomes for every student. The term *radical excellence* is defined as ambitious improvement and tireless focus for ensuring every student grows, thrives, and achieves to their fullest potential.

This book will provide district and school leaders with a bold blueprint for designing, implementing, and monitoring a comprehensive school improvement process that can lead to radical improvement. Examining questions like the ones posed will assist leaders and their teams in identifying the gaps that are keeping ambitious instruction out of reach for every type of student, including students with disabilities, students learning English, and those furthest away from ambitious learning. This book will focus on what works for all, and will specifically focus on students with disabilities because, for many, ambitious outcomes were out of reach before the pandemic and are even more so now.

For example, when the Supreme Court of the United States (SCOTUS) decided the landmark case *Endrew F. v. Douglas Co. School Dist. Re-1, 137*, in 2017, it ushered in a more substantive standard for ensuing students with disabilities were provided a free and appropriate public education. Despite the many articles and scholarly publications on the "higher standard," a separate lower standard has continued to persist for many students with complex needs. When I work with collaborative teams, I always ask *how* special education is represented within the collaborative team structure. Unfortunately, the majority of responses I receive include "They have their own meetings," or "Their schedules don't allow for them to attend," or "This is about regular education." This is simply unacceptable if all educators are responsible for the same thing—namely, improving outcomes for every student.

FRAGMENTATION

The current school improvement process is fragmented by policy, structure, and practice. I submit the current process had been fragmented long before the pandemic and it is exponentially so today. Unless daring action is taken, the trajectory of gaps may have a catastrophic effect for generations. That is a gamble I am not willing to take. To change the course of this trajectory, the school improvement process must shift from a siloed structure to a comprehensive one that intentionally situates students at the center of every decision and action—from the boardroom to the classroom.

To address these long-standing fragmentations, including those related to students with disabilities, this book will describe how the United States Supreme Court's decision in *Endrew F.* shifted the floor of education from a *de minimis* (just more than trivial) standard to a more substantive standard with shared accountability. This book will challenge district and school leaders to identify ways of comprehensively embedding special education programming and effective practices within the overall school improvement process. It will include suggested actions that districts and schools can take to meet the legal and ethical standards of the *Endrew F.* standard and the Individuals with Disabilities Education Act (IDEA, 2004), including how resources are determined, allocated, and monitored for impact. Why the focus on special education? Because when districts get that right—they get it right for every student.

A HIGHER STANDARD

To lay the groundwork for designing a comprehensive school improvement process, it is important to understand how the landmark case, *Endrew F. v. Douglas Co. School Dist. Re-1*, (2017) changed schools' legal and ethical responsibility for ensuring students with disabilities are provided an ambitious education.

BACKGROUND

In 2017, the Supreme Court of the United States unanimously decided the case of *Endrew F. v. Douglas County School District Re-1*. Depending on one's perspective, the ruling was either hailed for raising the standard of education for the wide spectrum of children with disabilities or it had little impact. Consider that it wasn't until the *Rowley* decision in 1982, that state education agencies and local school districts had to wrestle with what a free appropriate public education or FAPE meant. The *Rowley* standard required that school districts offer an Individualized Education Program (IEP) that was "appropriate" and "reasonably calculated to enable a child to receive educational benefit," such as, earning passing grades and grade advancement. But the *Rowley* decision did not substantively address the "how" for determining whether a FAPE was met. Further, the Court did not address the wide spectrum of students served under the Individuals with Disabilities Education Act (IDEA, 2004). Instead, the Court held that an IEP only needed to provide *some* benefit, meaning a *de minimis* standard or a "just more than trivial" education.

THE SHIFT

When the Supreme Court decided the *Endrew F. v. Douglas County School District Re-1* case, it clarified the *Rowley* standard and ushered in a broader vision by writing, "to meet its substantive obligation under the IDEA, a school must offer an IEP that is reasonably calculated to enable a child to make progress appropriate in light of the child's circumstances"; and that, "every child should have the chance to meet challenging objectives" (*Endrew F.*, 2017, p. 16)

The result of this decision for districts and schools meant a shift from a basic floor of education (*de minimis*) to being accountable for substantive progress for the wide spectrum of children served under the IDEA. Whereas *Rowley* was educated for the most part in the regular education setting, *Endrew F.* required more intensive academic and behavioral services. Thus, regardless of where a child sat on the continuum of disability, the Supreme Court's decision ushered in clear criteria that state education agencies, local school districts, charter schools, and other education organizations needed to consider.

The new standard included the following dimensions:

- Addressing the child's potential for growth
- Implementing an IEP that is reasonably calculated to enable the child to make progress in light of his/her circumstances
- Developing an IEP aligned to challenging standards
- Using a variety of data sources to determine the amount of progress
- Determining a FAPE via multiple data sources

WHY IT MATTERS

It is paramount that all educators understand that the federal education law, The Every Student Succeeds Act (2015), encompasses the needs of ALL students, meaning that a student with a disability is a regular education student first and foremost. Thus, the greatest opportunity to address the long-standing structural inequities that have kept many students, including students with disabilities, away from ambitious education is by dismantling the fragmented system and reengineering a comprehensive system that is correctly situated under the collective responsibility of the School Improvement Process.

It means that boards of education, district and school leaders, teachers, related service providers, and support staff work collaboratively rather than in isolation. It means implementing a comprehensive system of support (SoS) that encompasses flexible universal instruction with precision, recursive data analysis that supports the full spectrum of students, and effective academic and behavioral strategies implemented that surgically provides what students need in real time. It also means meeting the legal and ethical standards of special education, mitigating the effects of the pandemic, all of which can positively improve outcomes within and across the organization. This is the clarion call of our time.

CHAPTER ONE

THE SCHOOL IMPROVEMENT PROCESS UNPACKED

Without continual growth and progress,
such words as improvement, achievement,
and success have no meaning.

~ Ben Franklin

FIX THIS, CHANGE THAT

Ben sure had it right that without a focus on growth and progress, everything else is meaningless.

How many meetings have educators been in when this type of statement is uttered in the ethos?: "Our student assessment scores are bad, and we need to fix them." As if declaring it will magically reveal the land of absolute solutions. Instead, educators lower their heads, avoid eye contact, or look around the room searching for some external factor(s) to point to as the reason for the current state of affairs. Predictably this approach is guaranteed to fall short every single time. So, what approach does work? First, words like *bad* and *fix* should immediately be banned from the schools' lexicon. Second, help people understand what story the data is telling. Finally, get very clear on what a radically excellent school improvement process is—and what it is not.

WHAT ARE WE IMPROVING ANYWAY?

At the district level, a highly effective school improvement process [plan] should have a clearly articulated vision of aspiration and balanced reality based on data. It should be comprised of a tightly coordinated set of interdependencies across the organization, departments, and schools in a unified fashion. The goals should inform each school's plan by a cascading set of common expectations and structures so that effective practices can be implemented inside every classroom. Finally, shared accountability is the standard throughout the organization so that everyone can see themselves as being integral to the process and having ownership for every student.

This dynamic process is meant to keep people focused on the right efforts, but what often happens is that the plan falters after the first few steps. Take for example, the Janesville School District in Wisconsin. During a presentation at the What's Right in Education Gallery Walk in 2021, the leaders described the process used by their district and at each of their twenty-one schools. They described the six-step process (Diagnose, Plan, Implement, Monitor, Adjust, Reflect) and admitted "While [the] schools were great at the first three steps, . . . they struggled with revisiting their plan and monitoring progress to adjust throughout the year. Previously, plans were at least 20 pages long. Often, they sat in a folder unopened until the end of the year." The speakers went on to say that because each school used a different template, communication, collaboration, and implementation barriers occurred. These types of barriers are common across districts, and so using a common template is recommended to help with both form and function.

WHEN WE KNOW BETTER, WE HAVE THE OPPORTUNITY TO DO BETTER

An effective school improvement process will value interdependency as *the* way for catalyzing equity within and across the system. Moreover, interdependency will be understood to be the unifying foundation that will align and embed the work of the school improvement process. For example, the Human Resources Department could have a shared role with Teaching and Learning regarding the competencies needed to meet the needs of the students in the district. This could include working together on interview questions and the professional development calendar, as well as working with the collective bargaining units to ensure aligned understanding and agreement. This type of interdependency can create the opportunity for meeting the needs of the full continuum of students, including students with disabilities, through a set of strength-based principles, supports, resources, and practices. This dynamic and embedded process can also help meet the legal and ethical responsibilities for ensuring the higher *Endrew F.* (1982) standard.

THE ROOT OF THE ROOT

I have encountered various iterations of school improvement plans throughout my work with districts and state departments. Some have been conflated with strategic plans while others have been divorced from the work of education all together. I have also observed educators giving more deference to the template than the data used to inform the foci of the actual plan. Please don't make this mistake. Instead, keep a relentless focus on what matters.

To help teams get to the "root of the root" cause(s) that will inform their school improvement process, an equity analysis must be conducted. This analysis will get to the deep sources of the causal evidence that can lead toward or away from improving outcomes for every student. The Equity Audit is a that type of analysis. It is a quantitative and qualitative data gathering tool that can be used at the district and school level at the beginning of the process and also used as a dynamic monitoring tool. Remember that it is only through monitoring and adjustment that progress and growth are realized. The data gathering tool and accompanying guiding questions are included as an Appendix at the back of this book.

HOW TO

So how does a district or school get to the root of the root? The answer is straightforward, but it will demand courage by asking tough questions and by accepting the truths that are revealed. Resist the temptation to identify the cause during the first round of analysis. Instead go deeper with the analysis. Challenge the team from using the phrase, "The student…" to assign the reasons (causes) for the achievement results. Instead, have the team members ask this pivotal question, "How are the adults across the system and the practices within the classroom accounting for the data?" Using a carrot to illustrate this point, people might be satisfied when they pull up the root vegetable and never consider what contributed to it being delicious. So let's go deeper and find out. There was a whole network of roots deep below that supported the development of the carrot and even some that stunted its growth. The soil had the correct nutrients. There was sufficient water to quench the main roots as well as the ancillary root system, and a high-quality source of sunlight that fostered the conversion of sun to energy. All these factors enabled the carrot to thrive and grow. It is this level of analysis that members of the school improvement team should commit to perform so that a responsive and nimble improvement process can be reimagined and engineered. The root of the root figure (see Figure 1.1) illustrates the level of analysis needed to comprehensively align resources and interdependencies within and across the organization so that a cohesive process can be relentlessly designed, implemented, and used to grow students.

Figure 1.1 • *The root of the root*

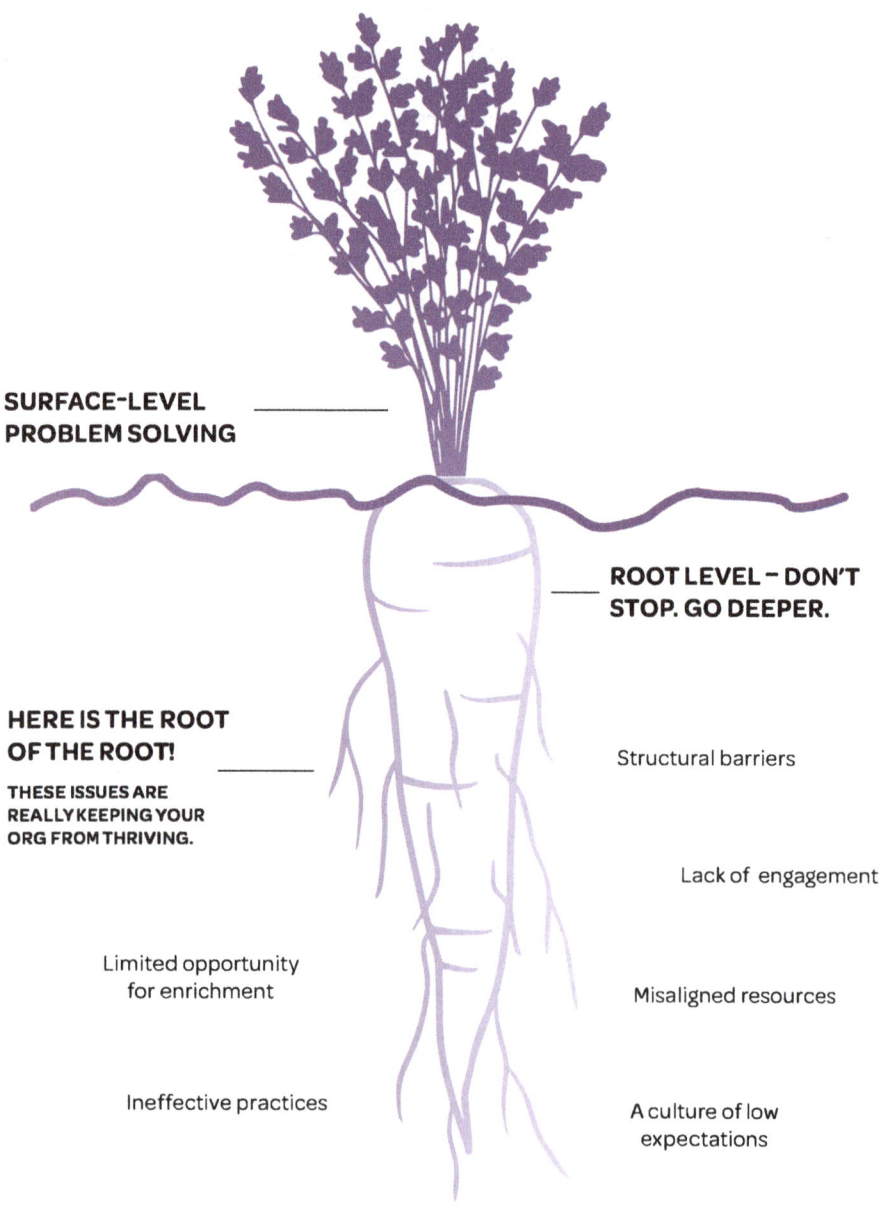

Source: Casi Hall Creative, LLC.

Here are the general steps of a root of the root analysis:

1. Collect the data for each condition of the Equity Audit.
2. Analyze what the causal data indicates.
3. Identify the root cause(s).
4. Don't stop! Ask deeper questions about the cause(s) for the causal data.
5. Identify the structural antecedents of the deeper causal data.
6. Identify one or two high-leverage actions that will address the antecedent causal data.

EXAMPLE

The following example illustrates how to conduct a root of the root analysis for the improvement process.

Academic Data of English Learner (EL) and Students With Disabilities (SWD)

- 76% of students limited or basic in reading
- 82% of students limited or basic in math
- Discipline referrals include a high number of cell phone use infractions
- High number of student absences for EL and SWD

Root Cause(s)

- There is a culture of low expectations
- Limited opportunity for enrichment
- Lack of student engagement

Root of the Root Cause(s)

- Remediation is the focus rather than acceleration
- Ability grouping is the structural policy and practice
- Lack of collaboration among teachers and related services for codesigning engaging lessons using relevant materials
- Lack of a nimble system of support

ANALYSIS

It may be tempting to say it is the students' fault for the low achievement data. They don't show up, they are on their cell phones during instruction, they are "EL and SWD." Resist this misplaced assumption. Instead, persist in examining why students aren't in class or why they are on their phones. Do students have the requisite skills? Students who don't possess the requisite background knowledge can lead to lack of engagement, being checked out inside or outside the classroom. Does *every single person* in the organization have high expectations for every student regardless of background or circumstance? If there is a culture of low expectations, especially for students furthest away from access and opportunity, then student growth will remain stagnant, and gaps will widen. Are there polices (structural antecedents) in place that are creating unrealistic constraints for providing high quality instruction? If pacing guides take precedence over meeting the basic needs of students, then there will be no sustainable improvement. By using the data from the Equity Audit, the district or school can identify the root of the root causes so that the right focused actions and supports can be implemented, monitored, and adjusted in real time.

THE FIVE CONDITIONS

The best way to get to those deeper root of the root causes is by using an equity audit such as the one provided at the back of this book. The purpose of the Equity Audit is to examine the level of implementation across the five conditions for creating a comprehensive school improvement process.

The five conditions for creating a comprehensive, equity-focused district and school improvement process include the following descriptions:

1. General and Social Characteristics
   The purpose of this condition is to understand the district as a whole. It provides a meaningful way to understand the context. It provides a connected understanding of who the students are and the educators who are responsible for ensuring learning.

2. Students
   The purpose is to measure the conditions under which students have access to high-quality educational and socioemotional instruction and supports. It examines the degree to which a high-quality, rigorous curriculum and a system of support is implemented within the classroom and across disciplines.

3. Practices
   The purpose of this condition is to understand the adult competencies related to the practices of teaching and learning, as well as socioemotional, cultural, and linguistic competencies to address opportunity gaps. It

identifies the effective practices that benefit all students, including students with disabilities.

4. Resources
   The purpose of this condition is to assess the human, fiscal, and material resources that support students, families, teachers, school, and district. It assesses the degree of aligned resources across and within the district and school(s).

5. Governance
   The purpose of this condition is to determine the alignment of governance across and within the system that support the development of teacher, principal, and district leadership.

Source: Equity Audit © included in the Appendix

Now it's your turn. Utilize the resources available across the district and within each department to complete the equity audit. Use the steps of the root of the root analysis to identify the true causes and structural inequities so that specific high-leverage actions can be taken. The results will serve as the foundations of your radically excellent school improvement process.

Turning Ideas Into Action

- Ask each member of the improvement team, to write down what's holding their school back from making radical improvement? Remember, the term *radical* is meant to convey ambitious improvement and a tireless focus for ensuring every student grows, thrives, and achieves.
- Commit to completing the Equity Audit. After completing the *General and Social Characteristics* condition, the team can go to its school's most pressing condition or simply complete it in order.
- Conduct a root of the root analysis of the data collected for each condition. Look for emergent trends across conditions.
- Identify two high-leverage actions that can focus the district and school improvement process on the right causal data. This data will be monitored and adjusted using real-time data on a routine basis and documented within a clear and dynamic improvement template.

CHAPTER TWO

THE HIGHER STANDARD

> When all is said and done, a student offered an educational program
> providing 'merely more than *de minimis'* progress from year
> year can hardly be said to have been offered an education at all. For
> children with disabilities, receiving instruction that aims so low
> would be tantamount to 'sitting idly … awaiting the time when
> they were old enough to drop out.'
>
> ~ Chief Justice Roberts

There are certain landmark cases that break through outdated ideas so new understandings can emerge. The *Endrew F.* decision in 2017 was that type of case. That decision effectively shifted the floor from a basic education for students served under the Individuals with Disabilities Education Act (IDEA 2004) to a more substantive responsibility for ensuring their education. To understand this shift, we must look back and understand how the Justices arrived at their decision. This figure illustrates the historical dimensions of special education that school districts are responsible for providing (Figure 2.1).

Before the Education for All Handicapped Children Act (EAHCA) of 1975 was enacted, many children with disabilities were denied entry to school and access to an education. Hence, the EAHCA opened the door to public education. Between 1975 and 1982, when the *Rowley* case was decided by the Supreme Court, many children sat isolated in restrictive settings and away from any meaningful educational opportunity. Then, in 1982, the *Board of Ed. of Hendrick Hudson Central School Dist., Westchester County v. Rowley* case was decided. The result of that decision established what is commonly referred to as the *Rowley* standard or *de minimis* standard. It meant that school districts across the country operated under the standard of "some" educational benefit for determining if a student with a disability had been provided a free and appropriate public education or a FAPE. As a result, school districts spent millions of dollars defending this *de minimums* standard which became the epitome of a siloed and fragmented system. Ask any parent if they'd be satisfied if their child received a "just more than trivial" education? Yet this was the accepted expectation for students with disabilities.

Figure 2.1 • *The evolution of special education law leading to* Endrew F. *decision*

Dimensions of Special Education	Brown v. Board Decision	Education of Handicapped Children Act	Rowley Decision	Individuals with Disabilities Education Act	*Endrew F.* Decision
	1954	1975	1982	1990	2017
Childs potential for growth					✔
Ambitious IEP					✔
Variety of data used to determine FAPE					✔
IEP aligned to academic materials				✔	✔
Goals resonably calculated			✔	✔	✔

Source: Casi Hall Creative, LLC.

A HIGHER STANDARD

For the next thirty-five years, students with disabilities experienced uneven access and opportunity to their education. As the figure illustrates, the *Endrew F.* Supreme Court decision of 2017 resulted in the 'higher' standard that we have today. This higher and more substantive standard called upon the education community to see students with disabilities as capable along with a shared responsibility for providing ambitious opportunities (Figure 2.2).

We can all agree that special education law can be intimidating but that doesn't give permission to ignore the fact that students with disabilities are first and foremost regular education students. The antidote to intimidation is education. So, district and school leaders, educators, and parents are encouraged to commit to becoming legally literate. Lean into the principles and intent of the law that should inform the school improvement process and that can proactively meet the needs of its students. School leaders can start with the unwavering acknowledgment that students with disabilities are first and foremost regular education students. That single nonnegotiable can lead to high expectations of the adults for students, and ambitious individual education programs (IEP) designed to address the gaps created by the disability. It would mean having a collaborative team structure that intentionally uses data to design instruction, intervention, and enrichment that leads to substantive progress. It would mean having a nimble system of support that includes every student and where effective strategies are delivered with precision with varying degrees of intensity inside the classroom rather than being sent away from the core instruction. These practices can benefit students who are underserved and in need of more help and can rightly provide the correct intervening strategies that narrow or eliminate gaps, which is also essential, so students are not inappropriately labeled with a disability. These structures also benefit students who are learning English as a second language, students who are at risk of failure, and students who may need accelerated learning opportunities. If this sounds like high-quality teaching, it is. When we get the condition of special education right, we get education right and all students win.

Now it's your turn. The data from the Equity Audit and the root of the root analysis will provide the areas of relentless focus, meaning the team is laser focused on the causes that are keeping students from growing, thriving, and achieving. When student outcomes improve, so does the school and district. Therefore, the next steps include examining the questions so a coherent and interdependent improvement process can begin to be reimagined. Pay particular

Figure 2.2 • *How* Endrew F. *shifted special education*

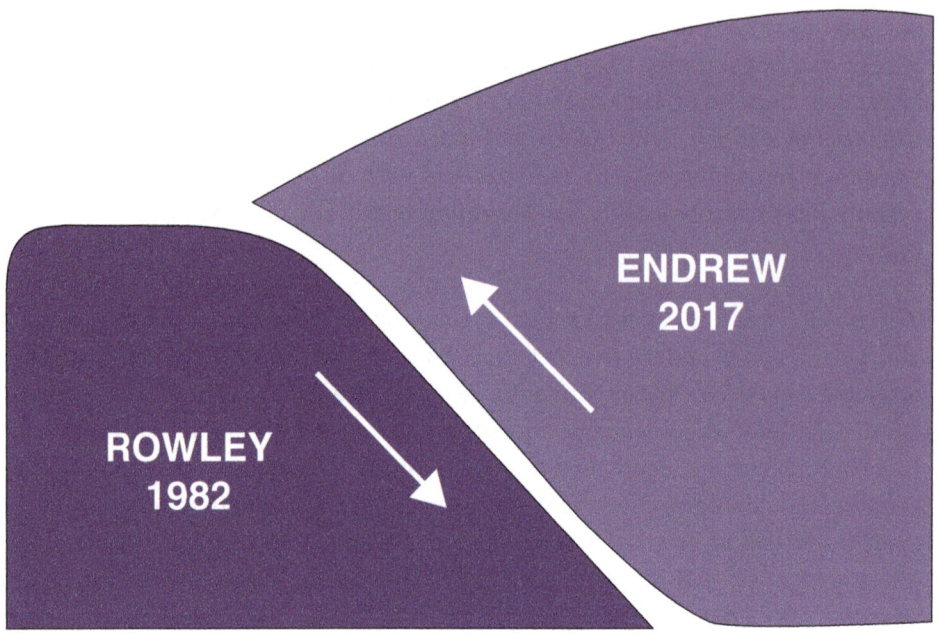

ROWLEY 1982	ENDREW 2017
• Established "some" educational benefit to determine FAPE • SEAS differed about the some vs meaningful standard • No one test to determine FAPE	• Substantive obligation for FAPE • Accountability for substantive progress • Prospective (fact-driven) IEP • IEP tailored to meet the unique needs of the student • Appropriately ambitious IEP • Still no one test to determine FAPE *(Need robust data system to do this effectively and minimize litigation.)*

Source: Casi Hall Creative, LLC.

attention to the structural inequities (the policies and institutional practices that are limiting or outdated yet still in place) that might be holding the district or school back from ensuring the higher standard is being met.

Turning Ideas Into Action

- Identity how the special education department is situated in the district. Is it a stand-alone department or is it a coequal partner with other the departments? Identify any interdependencies. If there aren't any, that is the data point that can be used in the imagine phase.
- What interdependencies exist between the Special Education and Teaching & Learning departments, including learners of English and students in advanced programs? Get to the root of the root.
- Does the district recognize the higher standard? What evidence leads to that conclusion? For example, are there written statements, policies, guidelines, and practices explicitly describing how the district will ensure it is being implemented?
- Do the IEPs reflect the higher *Endrew* standard? What evidence leads to that conclusion?
- What professional development related to the shift has been provided? Are teachers and staff supported with coaching to ensure deep implementation?
- Do schedules reflect the importance of codesign and coserving? This will help build the capacity for shared accountability.
- Identify two high-leverage actions for building the capacity of all educators, staff, and families to increase knowledge and skills of the higher standard.

CHAPTER THREE

THE DOUBLE HELIX SYSTEM OF SUPPORT

We thought that we had all the answers.
It was the questions we had wrong.

~ Bono

RAZZLE DAZZLE

Remember the courtroom scene in the musical production of Chicago? Attorney Billy Flynn, played by Richard Gere, is defending Roxie Hart who is accused of murdering her husband. He artfully pontificates and razzle dazzles the jurors to the point where they can no longer discern fact from fiction. That same clever showmanship is often employed in the name of improving conditions for students in today's schools. Dizzying amounts of information can be mind-numbing as vendors with sophisticated algorithms, software programs, and slick presentations proudly proclaim promises of increased student scores using the same seductive conviction as Billy Flynn in Chicago. In the wake of the pandemic and unprecedented federal relief funds, the promise of time-saving efficiencies for identifying students via targeted or strategic assessments and interventions are even more enticing. There are also vendors who describe response to intervention (RtI) and multi-tiered system of support (MTSS) as the same thing or, at best, interchangeable concepts. Don't be fooled by the show. They are not the same and while they may be contributors to the comprehensive system, accepting this unfounded razzle dazzle will not help our students.

RTI, IDEA, MTSS, ESSA, OH MY!

Response to Intervention emerged from the 2004 reauthorization of the Individuals with Disabilities Education Act (2004). The intent was to shift from the strict use of a discrepancy model for determining a learning disability to a more intervention-based approach (Zirkel, n.d.). The concept of multi-tiered system of support emerged out of the Every Student Succeeds Act of 2015, in its attempt to ameliorate persistent low-performing achievement across the nation. Furthermore, it addressed the behavioral aspects of learning that negatively impacted student outcomes. But as George Sugai, the preeminent authority on schoolwide positive behavior support, cautioned schools, "Label the interventions, not the students." Sugai further advocated that schools needed to get clear on what quality teaching and learning was and arrange support, so students could access their learning.

While RtI and MTSS are both worthy endeavors, the results of these systems have led to confusion and misinterpretation of intent, as well as misapplication of practices, instructional strategies, supports, and evidence of its intended impact. Instead, a false narrative that's based on external mechanisms and passive accountability via expensive programs with questionable fidelity have set the improvement process up for failure or best limited success. In fact, for many districts, these limiting frames simply became another pathway for referring students for special education. But here's the truth—the real magic. It's what happens *inside* the classroom that has the most impact. Put another way, effective teachers matter. Effective principals matter too. In fact, effective principals contribute to student achievement nearly as much as the average effects of teachers.

SAME THINKING WILL GET YOU THE SAME RESULTS

Districts and schools operating under the same tiered system that was in place before the pandemic, would be wise to reflect on the urban legend definition of insanity, namely, "doing the same thing over and over again and expecting different results." Said a different way, if what was in place before wasn't effective, what would lead one to think it will be different this time? If improvement is the goal, then grading, schedules, RtI, MTSS, and teacher practices must change. Now is the time to implement the principles of radical excellence with the first step being getting crystal clear on what is indispensable for educating the students in the wake of the pandemic and into the future.

LOSS OF ALL KINDS

The effects from the pandemic have been widely reported but there continues to be a lack of strategic direction to help district and school leaders think through the challenges of obsolete mind frames. Globally, it is estimated that eight million children, eighteen and younger, lost a parent or caregiver worldwide from the pandemic and over 250,000 of those are students in the United States. The social dimension of learning recognizes that more than one in 360 students lost a family member or caregiver. Thus, schools will need to align their systems of support to help ameliorate the exponentially high rates of anxiety and depression students are experiencing. Why does this matter? It matters, because students who have experienced such loss and trauma often exhibit similar behaviors as students with disabilities, such as distractedness, short attention span, difficulty understanding or expressing thoughts (verbally or written), verbal or physical outbursts, avoidance, and many others. In fact, over 80% of public school districts have reported that the pandemic has had a negative impact on behavior, discipline, and the social development of children and youth.

I remember when I had my first experience witnessing how trauma can lay dormant until a triggering event happens that causes the person to instinctively react. I was in the second grade during the Vietnam War. I remember a young father who was a white American veteran, and the mother who was Vietnamese, enter the classroom with their child taking a tour of what would become her new world. The next day she arrived, and we all welcomed her and the teacher began teaching. When it was time for our lavatory break, we all dutifully proceeded to our assigned lines. I remember taking our new classmate, so she'd learn the routine. All went well until we returned to the classroom. My new friend was making her way to her desk when a boy bounded through the doorway yelling "AHHH!" That was the trigger that caused my new friend to freeze, hold her hands to her face, cry, and divebomb under her desk. She was instantly thrown back to a physically and psychologically unsafe place and she reacted the only way she could. *Run! Hide! Survive!* At that moment, I felt what she was feeling, and it shifted something inside of me that has stayed with me. I learned later that "core shift" was perspective. I share this story because there are many students who come to school wearing their invisible backpacks of trauma who we need to acknowledge and be responsive to. Why does this matter? It matters because by understanding our students at their core, for who they are and what they carry with them into the schoolhouse, provides the pathways that can make learning accessible for every student. The acknowledgment that there has been loss of all kinds, puts a human face on how schools can be responsive while holding high expectations that every student is capable of learning as the nonnegotiable belief.

We've also seen the effects across reading and mathematics scores that show several months of learning loss in reading and even more in mathematics (National Assessment of Educational Progress, 2023). The results are even more bleak for students with complex needs, including students who are learning English, students from economically disadvantaged communities, and students with disabilities (Figure 3.1).

Figure 3.1 • *NAEP long-term trend assessment result: Reading and mathematics*

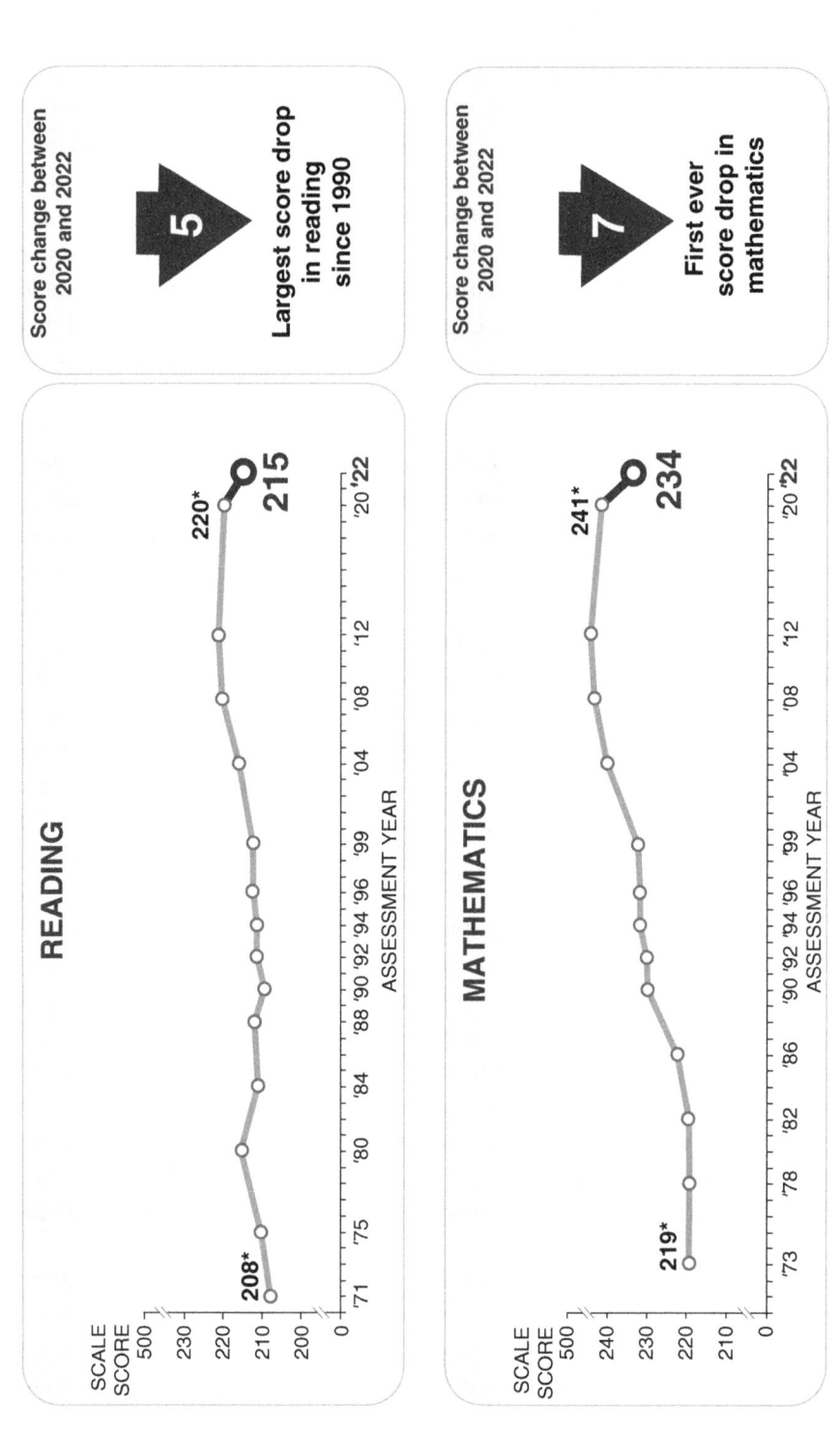

Source: National Assessment of Educational Progress (2023).

WHEN WE GET THE QUESTIONS RIGHT, EVERYONE WINS

So, if students present differently as a result of the pandemic, shouldn't the educational system respond differently? If there was nothing holding your team back from designing a comprehensive system that works in conjunction with the improvement process, what would it be?

Think about the current system where the tringle is displayed like this △ or like ▽ this. Regardless of where the tip points, the assumption is the process funnels one way toward the tip. However, this type of support structure is still insufficient for describing how schools can improve outcomes for students because it is based on the concept of linear directionality. Instead of a triangle, consider a double helix to represent the system of support. Each strand serves as the complementary backbone of the other, creating a complete structure. The elements are nondirectional, and yet absolutely dependent upon the whole, creating a cohesive system. In other words, when the structural conditions are right—everyone in the system thrives. Students along the full continuum of learning, for example, can engage with ambitious content, supported by real-time differentiated instruction and scaffolded supports, and teachers have the right data to take actionable next steps (Figure 3.2).

The elements of the Double Helix System of Support are intentionally designed to achieve a comprehensive approach to the very real concerns of supporting all students including those furthest away from meeting the established academic and social emotional dimensions of learning and accountability. The Double Helix is designed to serve as that foundation for the overall school improvement process because it places students at the center of every point along the decision-making process. This means there are high expectations of the educational, financial, and human resources to intentionally align and allocate all recourses in a coordinated and aligned manner within and across the organization and inside every classroom. This strength-based approach can meet the needs of all students, including those with complex needs including disability.

Here are the structural elements of the Double Helix that defines the holistic strength-based system of support:
A Clear Definition: A nimble and responsive system of support (SoS) which encompasses the academic and social dimensions of learning serves as the overarching frame. Nimble means it is easily adaptive. Responsive means

Figure 3.2 • *Double Helix System of Support*

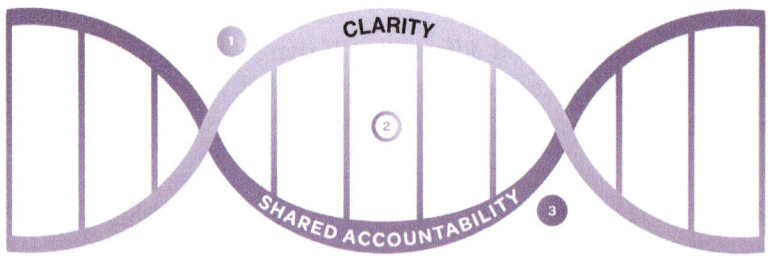

1

CLARITY

A strength-based system of support is the foundation for the broader school improvement process by supporting all learners and for ensuring equitable access to a high-quality education.

- A nimble and responsive system is defined for growth, support, and achievement
- High expectations by the adults are evident
- Accountability is measured by evidence of impact

2

DESIGN FEATURES

The tiers are banned and replaced with effective instruction, intervention, and acceleration practices delivered with precision and in real time.

- Staff are comprehensively situated inside the classroom
- Nimble and responsive strategies are delivered with precision
- Interventions are identified not students
- Data is used to inform, monitor, and adjust
- Indicators are used to monitor growth

3

SHARED ACCOUNTABILITY

Shared accountability is non-negotiable.

- Interdependencies are anchored to the improvement process
- Adult competencies are strategically supported
- Academic and social dimensions of learning are delivered with precision
- A collaborative team structure is deeply implemented and is responsible for all students

Source: Casi Hall Creative, LLC.

supports are provided in real time. It provides the foundation for the broader school improvement process by supporting all learners and ensuring equitable access to high-quality education.

Shared Accountability: Implementation is the collective responsibility of all educators, staff, families, and communities. The adult skills needed for meeting the wide continuum of learners is provided by, supported, and monitored by district and school leadership teams. That means a productive collaborative team structure whereby all educators are comprehensively situated for the maximum benefit of all students.

Design: High expectations of the adults working with students is nonnegotiable. A nimble design enables educators to make data-informed decisions that meet the needs of students from different backgrounds, levels of language proficiency, learning complexities, and levels of attainment. Strategies that address needs are identified. Academic and behavioral instruction and support are implemented with stretch inside the classroom. The tiers formerly used to label students would be banned.

Here is an example of how one school district utilized the Double Helix System of Support as the foundation for their improvement process based on the findings of their Equity Audit and root of the root analysis of the *Students* and *Practices* conditions. The teaching and learning domain of the plan for ambitious education was supported by staff being comprehensively situated to where the students were receiving their instruction inside the classroom. It then cascaded to the adult supports aimed at building the capacity for deep implementation of those effective practices that were delivered in real time. Finally, it cascaded to shared accountability through a collaborative team structure. Taken together, these strategies supported a comprehensive approach for ensuring every student was part of the whole, along with the desired structural supports to make the shift from teaching in isolation to teaching collaboratively so that every student could experience a high-quality, ambitious education in a social and emotionally safe environment.

Domain: Teaching & Learning

Goal: Every student will experience a high-quality, ambitious education in a social and emotionally safe environment.

Strategic Actions

1. Implement the Double Helix System of Support with fidelity to create safe and engaging learning environments for all students. Related service providers (i.e., social workers, counselors, intervention specialists) will codesign and codeliver effective instruction that improves school culture and provides student supports in real time.

2. Implement proven social and emotional and strategies across learning environments so that academic growth can be accessed and achieved.

   - Develop teacher training with instructional coaching to ensure consistent implementation in each classroom.
   - Implement instructional coaching cycles. Schedule will be developed, and impact will be monitored by the each school improvement team.

3. Implement structured collaboration teams across grade levels. Each school will develop a bell schedule that reflects the collaboration team meetings within the school day. Each collaboration will be responsible for the following cycle of inquiry: Identify what students need to learn per unit of instruction. Analyze formative student assessments to determine if students have met the success criteria. Identify, implement, and monitor effective instructional strategies for students who haven't achieved mastery yet. Identify, implement, and monitor scaffolded rigor for students who have already mastered the content. Each collaboration team will document their weekly meetings and progress using a universally shared template. The meeting notes will be uploaded to a shared folder and available to the administration and the school improvement team.

Measurable Indicators

1. Fidelity the Double Helix System of Support will be provided through written guidelines, restructured bell schedules, and by comprehensively situating the adults who are responsible for ensuring learning. The number of students being referred for special education eligibility will be monitored in accordance with all legal timelines and responsibilities. Professional development, including effective and responsive practices, and the instructional coaching model will be implemented and monitored for effectiveness and reported on a trimester basis.

2. Social and emotional strategies will result in increased student engagement (from established baseline at each school and established trimester growth metric) and decreased number of students requiring out-of-classroom discipline. Student surveys measuring feelings of

inclusion, respect, belonging, and safety will be completed each trimester. The board of education will be provided updates at the end of each trimester.

3. Implementing a collaborative team structure will result in an increased number of students accessing ambitious instruction and receiving real-time supports inside the classroom. It will decrease the number of students being removed from their grade-level instruction to receive disparate supports that may or may not be aligned to what is being taught at that time. Educators will utilize the decisions made collectively during the collaboration meetings to design, implement, and assess growth via short cycle and formative assessment. This will be monitored on a weekly basis by collaborative team facilitators, instructional coaches, the principal, and the school improvement team.

Interdependencies

1. Site leadership, district leadership from the departments of Teaching & Learning, English Learners, Special Education, Human Resources, Business, and Information Technology, and the committee chair (s) from the Board of Education.

2. Site leadership, district leadership from the departments of Teaching & Learning, English Learners, Special Education, Human Resources, Business, and Information Technology, and the committee chair(s) from the Board of Education.

3. Site leadership, district leadership from the departments of Teaching & Learning, English Learners, Special Education, Human Resources, Business, and Information Technology, and the committee chair(s) for the Board of Education.

Now is the time to move away from the outdated, linear systems that perpetuate limiting mind frames and practices. It is time to rethink what it means to support the academic and social dimensions of learning so all students can grow, thrive, and achieve. It's time to ask the radical excellence question: If there was nothing holding your team back from designing a comprehensive system that works in conjunction with the improvement process, what would it be?

Now it's your turn. Your school improvement team is positioned for radical excellence which means a relentless focus on those systems and practices that will ensure all students grow, thrive, and achieve. Using the data from the *Students* and *Practices* conditions of the Equity Audit, and the results of the root of the root analysis, start to build out the school improvement process. Pay particular attention to how and where students who are furthest away from ambitious instruction are currently receiving their education, including students who are learning English and students with disabilities. The same ambitious academic and social emotional opportunities need to be afforded to every student regardless of where they sit on the continuum of learning.

Turning Ideas Into Action

- Complete the *Students* and *Practices* conditions of the Equity Audit to determine how effective the current structure of support is. Identify what's working.
- Identify what is not working and give permission to stop doing it.
- Ask this radical excellence question: If there was nothing holding your team back from designing a comprehensive system that works in conjunction with the improvement process, what would it be? Name it.
- Identify two high-leverage actions that can address existing barriers so that a comprehensive system of support can be designed as the foundation of your school improvement process.

CHAPTER FOUR

THE PARETO PRINCIPLE

For many events, roughly 80% of the effects
come from 20% of the causes.

~ Vilfredo Pareto

The Pareto Principle, also known as the 80–20 rule, states that 80% of the output from a situation or system is determined by 20% of the input. This inverse cause and effect relationship has been widely applied to business, economics, management, and education. However, it would be misleading to think that schools only needed to choose 20% of the standards or curriculum and forget the rest. But it does provide context for an improvement process that is laser-focused on those efforts (practices) that will have the most impact for ensuring student growth and achievement and improved schools.

INSIDE OUT CHANGE

The most powerful way to improve outcomes for students is through the adults in the system. But this inside out change is dependent upon getting the conditions right. Like concentric circles with students at its core (Figure 4.1), the next step of the process is to build upon what the team identified in the *Students* and *Practices* conditions of the Equity Audit and root of the root analysis, and the reimagined Double Helix System of Support, to flesh out the comprehensive improvement process at the district and school level.

Once the improvement team has identified those high impact key practices, and causal inputs that can yield the greatest desired effects, the team should examine the *Resources* and *Governance* conditions which assesses the human, fiscal, and material resources that support students, teachers families school, and the district as a whole. Intentionally aligning resources and governance structures, the improvement process can proactively support students' academic and socioemotional learning and systematically provide the needed supports for the educators within and across the organization.

Figure 4.1 • *Students at the center of it all*

Source: Casi Hall Creative, LLC.

But how will educators know that what they are doing inside the classroom is effective? The answer is straightforward yet ambitious. It can be done through the implementation of a collaborative team structure.

PROFESSIONALS WORKING TOGETHER

The top experts on collaborative teams describe their purpose in two important interconnected ways. Dr Douglas Reeves emphasizes that, "when educators work together in collaborative teams rather than in isolation, a collective responsibility for student learning is established." That collective responsibility for learning complements what John Hattie describes as the fundamental purpose of education, namely, "to ensure that students learn and not merely that they are taught." In the wake of the pandemic and the higher standard for students with disabilities and the needs of students with other complex needs, it will be imperative that leadership establish and intentionally support collaboration over isolation. The best way to do that is by professionals working together.

To that end, the next action in developing a comprehensive improvement process that meets the needs of all students, and by extension the adults, will be by reviewing the collaborative structure currently in place using the data collected from the *Practice, Resource,* and *Governance* conditions of the Equity Audit. This qualitative and quantitative data will provide important context for the improvement team as it determines the effectiveness of the collaborative structure at the district and school level. It will be essential to get to the root of the root for each condition because it will reveal valuable information about beliefs that adults hold, levels of implementation, and the evidence of impact to monitor improvement.

CLARITY IS THE NORTH STAR

That same relentless improvement mindset should also apply to the district and schools' pursuit of radical excellence. If nothing was holding team members back, how would the district and school improve upon its existing collaborative team structures?

Clarity of purpose is the north star when determining what students need to learn and what evidence that will be used to determine if they have learned it. Getting clear and get precise will be that north star. There are not enough hours in the day or weeks in the year to teach all the standards; thus, it will be critically important to identify those standards that have power and stretch to go the distance. Power and stretch means identifying the standards that are foundational for scaffolding to higher and more complex skills that students will need for the next unit of instruction, across content areas, and that inform vertical alignment. For example, what English Language Arts standard(s) are required to improve comprehension and written expression of nonfiction text for the third–fifth grade band? Using this as the example, the standard(s) for reading nonfiction text and responding to a persuasive writing prompt requires the student to cite evidence to justify their position will be used. Those same standard(s) can be applied across content, grades, and can provide the stretch for adapting instruction. By using engaging nonfiction texts and relevant writing prompts, teachers can make persuasive writing and evidence-based reasoning accessible and impactful across grade levels and across content areas. They can tailor the strategies to match where students currently are and to the next level of scaffolded instruction, while challenging them to think critically and to express their knowledge effectively.

This example illustrates how a collaboration team adapted nonfiction persuasive writing across content and across the grade levels for the students. Each prompt was universally designed so that every student could *engage* with the content (standard) in multiple ways through *representation*, and differentiated ways for *expressing* what they knew (mastery). Utilizing the principles of universal design, engagement, representation, and expression, coupled with differentiation, provided a strength-based approach that viewed students as capable while intentionally scaffolding learning so the full continuum of students could demonstrate growth in a psychologically safe environment. This approach is the type of nimble and responsive instruction that has stretch.

COLLABORATION TEAM

Lower Grades (K–2):

Reading: Picture books on environmental topics like recycling or saving water.

Writing Prompt: Should your class get a recycling bin? Use facts from the book to convince your classmates.

Differentiation: Younger students or students who are still developing written expression can draw pictures with captions to support their point. Older students can write short sentences with direct quotes from the story. Students who are advanced can write more complex sentences that convey their position. Students learning English can use voice to text translation so that the concepts can be evaluated versus the acquisition of language. Differentiation can be further customized based on individual student needs and learning styles.

Middle Grades (3–5):

Reading: Articles on historical figures who overcame challenges, like Rosa Parks or Malala Yousafzai.

Writing Prompt: Do schools need stricter rules against bullying? Use evidence from the article to explain your position.

Differentiation: Students can create graphic representations to analyze the reasons for and against stricter rules, citing specific examples from the article. Advanced students can write a persuasive letter to the school principal, using quotes and statistics. Students learning English can use voice recording to interview a another language peer. The recording can be translated to English so that the concepts can be evaluated versus the acquisition of language. This will make the content engaging and relevant and help the student persist learning the English language. Differentiation can be further customized based on individual student needs and learning styles.

Upper Grades (6–8):

Reading: Scientific articles on complex topics like climate change or renewable energy.

Writing Prompt: Should renewable energy sources be mandatory? Use data and research from the article to argue your position.

Differentiation: Students can write an editorial for the school newspaper, using rhetorical devices and counterarguments to strengthen their position. Advanced students can create a multimedia presentation with using charts and graphs to support their claims. Students learning English can choose how they want to demonstrate understanding. Ownership over the product will allow for the use of assistive technology while accurately assessing the success criteria. Differentiation can be further customized based on individual student needs and learning styles.

High School (9–12):

Reading: Literary criticism or historical primary sources on controversial topics like war or social justice.

Writing Prompt: Should social media platforms be held responsible for spreading misinformation? Analyze sources from different perspectives to justify your stance.

Differentiation: Students can write a formal argumentative essay with counterarguments using correct citations. Advanced students can engage in a debate where they defend their position using evidence from various sources. Students learning English can choose how they want to demonstrate understanding in accordance with the established rubric. Ownership over the product will allow for the use of assistive technology while accurately assessing the success criteria. Differentiation can be further customized based on individual student needs and learning styles.

Source: Kate Anderson Foley.

The examples illustrated that when educators were clear about what students needed to learn, the collaborative team could rightly focus on the types of evidence (student work) that were used to evaluate if students had learned and not merely that they were taught. They formatively assessed the skills and provided feedback to students so they could correct misunderstandings. The evidence was used to inform the recursive cycle of analysis whereby team members identified which strategies to implement for their students who hadn't mastered the skill *yet,* as well as strategies for extending the standard for students who already knew it.

This chapter provided the contours for what responsive ambitious education can achieve. The collective practice and strategies provided inside the classroom with precision and can empower educators to design to the edges. The result is student growth and achievement. This is the Pareto Principle.

The following chapters will delve into the ways of meeting the needs of all students, and specifically students with disabilities and how to implement the higher standard. But now it is your turn to reflect on what the data from the full Equity Audit and root of the root analysis have revealed. Use the elements of the Double Helix System of Support and continue to strategically reengineer the school improvement plan. Then ask these radical excellence questions to make sure all students are situated at the center of it all.

Turning Ideas Into Action

- If there were nothing holding your improvement team back from reimagining a district and school collaborative team structure, what would it be? Get specific.
- What needs to happen for this reimagined structure to be successful? Name it.
- How can schedules, classes, and common planning time be intentionally reengineered?
- Identify two actions that district and school leadership teams can commit to that will advance the deep implementation of a collaborative team structure.

CHAPTER FIVE

COACHING IS THE CONNECTING FIBER OF IMPROVEMENT

> Coaching done well may be the most effective intervention designed for human performance.
>
> ~ Atul Gawande

Congratulations! Bold and decisive actions have been taken to design an improvement process that meets the academic and social dimensions of your education organization. Your district and school plans are explicit, aligned, concise, and the interdependencies across the departments have been explicitly identified and codified. Now it is time to weave the interdependent practice of coaching into the comprehensive improvement process. Like the concentric circles (Figure 4.1), where coaching was situated between students and collaboration teams, coaching can serve as the connecting fiber between aligned professional practices of teachers and leaders, effective instructional and behavioral practices, including the higher *Endrew F.* standard, and a true system of support.

Coaching directly informs the improvement process in real time, so course corrections can be made within and across all levels of the organization. Coaching is a highly effective practice with tangible results. District and school leaders who have implemented coaching as an improvement strategy, shifted the focus from individual performance to one with a collective impact. Therefore, implementing a comprehensive coaching model should include BOTH instructional coaching and leadership coaching with explicitly referenced links to the district improvement process and school improvement process, along with how coaching will be implemented within and across the organization. Let's begin with instructional coaching.

INSTRUCTIONAL COACHING

The most valuable resource that all teachers have is each other.
Without collaboration our growth is limited to our own perspectives.

~ Robert John Meehan

An instructional coaching model connects the school's improvement plan, to the effective instructional practices that happen inside the classroom, with the work of the collaborative team structure. The role of an instructional coach should include a clearly defined job description, be transparent, is nonevaluative of teachers, and includes direct metrics that align to the school's plan for improving outcomes for students. While descriptions of instructional coaches vary, the must-haves should include a description of what instructional coaching is and what it is not. For example, instructional coaching should be a nonevaluative partnership between the teacher and coach that is based upon mutual respect within a safe and supportive environment. The role of the instructional coach is to intentionally scaffold the pedological knowledge and skills of teachers in order to better meet the academic and social dimensions of learning, and uses data effectively to inform the instructional and behavioral strategies that can lead to student growth. Having a clear job description of the desired qualities of an instructional coach can lead to securing a strong cadre of professional practitioners. Here are some qualities to look for when selecting an instructional coach. They represent the knowledge, skills, and depositions needed to evident in the performance of this role.

Qualities of an Effective Instructional Coach

- Possesses an ethical character
- Relentlessly focused on academic and socioemotional student growth
- Demonstrates data literacy
- Demonstrates cultural competency
- Demonstrates knowledge of the school improvement process and how to coach to it
- Demonstrates skills to scaffold adult learning
- Effective use of coaching questions
- Feedback given that results in reflection and action
- Implements coaching cycles that align to need and improvement targets
- Demonstrates knowledge and skills to support collaboration teams
- Demonstrates skills to effectively coach the delivery of rigorous and relevant content and tailored support inside the classroom
- Demonstrates knowledge and skills for building shared accountability within and across departments of a school or district

- Creates a safe and supportive working relationship with teachers and collaborative teams
- Relies on evidence to inform instructional practices (academic/behavioral)
- Uses evidence to evaluate their own impact on teacher growth
- Collaboratively identifies evidence used to evaluate teacher impact on student growth
- Demonstrates ability to see the big picture as well as the discrete parts of the improvement process

An equally important consideration for implementing an instructional coaching model is identifying the evidence that will be used to measure their collective impact. An effective instructional coaching model strategically supports schools by linking the continuous improvement process to equity, instructional and behavioral practices, collaboration, and feedback. This evidence should align to the work of the teacher collaborative team structure—for example, the standard for a unit of instruction, the criteria that will be used to determine student success, the data to evaluate class and individual mastery, and the strategies that will be used to scaffold gaps or extend learning.

Finally, it will be important that the instructional coaches establish themselves with the building leadership, provide regular updates on progress, create a calendar for implementing coaching cycles, list the protocols that will be used to document their work, and the processes for how the data will be used to inform the collaborative team meetings, system of support, students individual education programs, and the recursive cycle for reporting school improvement efforts.

The following case study highlights one school's successful implementation of an instructional coaching model, demonstrating the positive impact on teachers, students, and the overall school improvement process.

CASE STUDY

Implementing an Instructional Coaching Model at Ida B. Wells Elementary

Background: Ida B. Wells Elementary is a public school in a diverse urban community, serving students from various socioeconomic backgrounds. The school has shown consistent commitment to student success, but the administration recognized the need for a structured approach to professional development and support for teachers. In response, the leadership team decided to implement an instructional coaching model to enhance teaching practices and promote a culture of continuous improvement.

Objective: The primary objective of implementing instructional coaching at Ida B. Wells Elementary was to elevate teaching quality, foster collaboration among educators, and ultimately improve student outcomes. The coaching model aimed to provide personalized support to teachers, focusing on areas such as equity, continuous improvement, collaboration, and effective feedback.

Implementation Steps

1. Needs Assessment

   • The Equity Audit was used to identify the specific challenges faced by teachers and areas that needed improvement.

   • Analyzed student performance data, teacher surveys, and feedback from previous professional development initiatives.

2. Selection of Coaches

   • Identified experienced and skilled teachers with a proven track record of success in the classroom.

   • Ensured that the selected coaches possessed strong interpersonal skills, a commitment to equity, and a deep understanding of effective teaching practices.

3. Professional Development for Coaches

   • Provided comprehensive training for coaches, focusing on the coaching model, equity principles, data analysis, and effective communication strategies.

   • Emphasized the importance of creating a supportive and nonjudgmental coaching environment.

4. Implementation Plan

   • Gradually introduced the coaching model, starting with a pilot phase involving a small group of teachers.

   • Gathered feedback from both teachers and coaches to make necessary adjustments before expanding the program schoolwide.

5. Equity Integration

   • Emphasized the importance of equity in coaching sessions, ensuring that coaches were equipped to address disparities in student outcomes.

   • Coaches guided teachers in creating inclusive lesson plans and adapting instructional strategies to meet the diverse needs of students.

6. Continuous Improvement Cycles

- Established regular data review cycles to identify trends, assess the impact of coaching interventions, and make data-informed decisions.
- Encouraged teachers to reflect on their own practices and set goals for continuous improvement.

7. Collaboration and Communities of Practice

- Facilitated collaboration among teachers through the formation of communities of practice (i.e., teacher-based teams).
- Coaches supported the communities of practice (teacher-based teams) by sharing best practices, discussing challenges, sources of evidence that can be used formatively, and collectively working toward common goals.

8. Feedback and Reflection

- Implemented a robust feedback system where coaches provided timely, specific, and actionable feedback to teachers.
- Encouraged teachers to reflect on feedback and set goals for ongoing professional growth.

Outcomes:

- Improved teacher efficacy and confidence.
- Enhanced collaboration and a sense of community among educators.
- Increased student engagement and achievement, particularly for historically marginalized groups.
- Positive shifts in school culture toward a more reflective and growth-oriented mindset.

LEADERS AS COACHES

Coaching is one of the most effective leadership styles that can transform, empower, and unlock people's potential.
Ask more, give advice less, and elevate your impact forever.

~ Farshad Asl

The role of principal has moved far beyond that of manager, if it ever was just that, yet not enough attention has been paid to comprehensively building the knowledge, skills, and dispositions to support this role. The impact of leadership is so influential that the authors of the 2004 report on how principals effect schools and student outcomes wrote, "Leadership is second only to classroom instruction among all school-related factors that contribute to what students learn at school" (Leithwood et al., 2004, p. 5). The findings were so important that the Wallace Foundation (Grissom et al., 2021) commissioned a study in 2021 that synthesized over two decades of research on the effects. Among the findings, the authors found that, "Across six rigorous studies estimating principals' effects using panel data, principals' contributions to student achievement were nearly as large as the average effects of teachers identified in similar studies. Principals' effects, however, are larger in scope because they are averaged over all students in a school, rather than a classroom."

Leadership coaching provides the necessary knowledge, skills, and dispositions so that leaders across the organization can pivot to "leader as coach." How one builds these professional practices is just as important as the practices themselves. The Effective Principal (Figure 5.1) illustrates the relationship of the competencies needed to be an effective leader, and in turn, to be a leader as coach.

The practices of an effective principal as coach includes the ability to create an atmosphere of purposeful engagement, build a positive school culture, implement a collaborate team structure, and manage resources strategically.

The same competencies that principals need to possess also apply to district-level leaders; thus, the moral imperative is to carefully select an external coaching team that has the breadth and depth of practice that will result in true transformation. This author cannot think of any other group other than her own (www.edpolicyconsulting.com) than that of Creative Leadership Solutions, where they are dedicated to evidence-based coaching with embedded professional learning that catalyze improvement. Moreover, this organization has invested an abundance of resources to ensure its leadership coaches are skilled in performance coaching and have access to the latest research. Such a commitment can translate to providing results-based coaching that leads to a sustainable practice across the organization. For more information and immediate useable resources, this author, who was a contributor, strongly suggests obtaining the book *Fearless Coaching* (Reeves, 2023).

https://qrs.ly/25fii08

To read a QR code, you must have a smartphone or tablet with a camera. We recommend that you download a QR code reader app that is made specifically for your phone or tablet brand.

Figure 5.1 • *The effective principal*

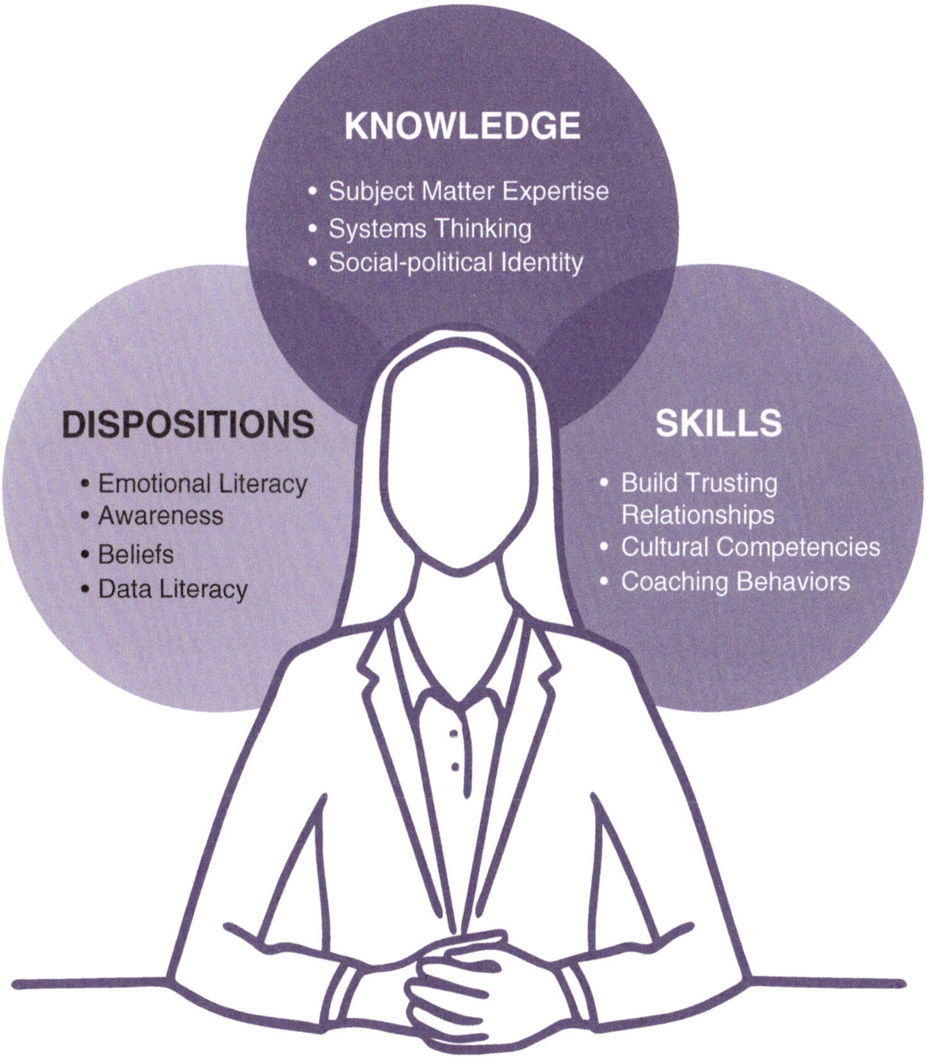

KNOWLEDGE
- Subject Matter Expertise
- Systems Thinking
- Social-political Identity

DISPOSITIONS
- Emotional Literacy
- Awareness
- Beliefs
- Data Literacy

SKILLS
- Build Trusting Relationships
- Cultural Competencies
- Coaching Behaviors

Source: Casi Hall Creative, LLC.

The following case study highlights how one school district successfully implemented leadership coaching for both school principals and central office administrators. It demonstrates how a holistic coaching approach contributed to a thriving culture of educational excellence and continuous improvement.

CASE STUDY

Implementing Leadership Coaching for Principals and Central Office Administrators in Manchester School District.

Background: The Manchester School District is a suburban district with a focus on student achievement and recognized the pivotal role of school principals and central office administrators in driving systemic improvement. To enhance leadership effectiveness, the district decided to implement a comprehensive leadership-coaching program tailored for both principals and central office administrators.

Objective: The primary objective of implementing leadership coaching was to empower and support school principals and central office administrators in their leadership roles, fostering a culture of continuous improvement and student success.

Implementation Steps

1. Needs Assessment

   • Conducted an Equity Audit to identify leadership strengths, areas for growth, and specific challenges faced by principals and central office administrators.

   • Gathered input from administrators, teachers, and staff to ensure a well-rounded understanding of the district's needs.

2. Selection of Coaches

   • Identified a team of experienced leadership coaches with expertise in educational leadership and coaching.

   • Coaches were selected based on their ability to build strong relationships, understand the unique challenges of school leadership, and align with the district's values.

3. Onboarding for Coaches

   • Coaches attended an onboarding session that incorporated the district's leadership framework, emphasizing the alignment with district goals and the importance of collaborative leadership.

   • Onboarding consisted of modules on equity, effective communication, and data-informed decision-making.

4. Dual Focus on Principals and Central Office Administrators

   • Coordinated coaching efforts for both school principals and central office administrators, recognizing the interconnectedness of their roles in advancing districtwide goals.

   • Coaches tailored their approaches to address the specific needs and responsibilities of each group and aligned them to the district improvement process.

5. Individualized Coaching Goals

   • Coaches collaborated with each principal and central office administrator to develop individualized coaching goals with benchmarks and metrics for success.

   • Goals included targeted goals aligned with district priorities, strategies for leadership development, and measurable outcomes.

6. Equity Integration

   • Infused an equity focus into coaching sessions, guiding administrators in addressing equity gaps within their schools and departments.

   • Coaches supported the development and implementation of strategies to promote the academic and social dimensions of learning in culturally responsive ways.

7. Continuous Improvement Monitoring

   • Established regular feedback loops and reflection sessions to monitor the impact of coaching.

   • Coaches and administrators collaboratively assessed progress, adjusted goals as needed, and celebrated successes.

8. Cross-Collaboration Initiatives

   • Facilitated cross-collaboration initiatives between principals and central office administrators.

- Coaches encouraged shared leadership, effective communication, and collaborative problem-solving to strengthen the overall district leadership team.

Outcomes:

- Enhanced leadership skills among school principals and central office administrators.
- Improved alignment of leadership practices with district goals and priorities.
- Increased collaboration and interdependency between school and central office leadership.
- Positive impact on student achievement, school and district culture, and shared accountability for the improvement process.

Now it's your turn. Reflect on the ways instructional coaching and leadership coaching can serve as the connecting fiber for improving outcomes for students. Those connecting fibers can support the people whose responsibility it is for ensuring improvement from the classroom to the boardroom. That is shared accountability at its best.

Turning Ideas Into Action

- Ask this radical excellence question: If nothing was holding your team back from improving outcomes for every student, what steps would need to be taken to implement a comprehensive coaching model across the organization?
- How can the human, fiscal, and material resources be aligned to support the deep implementation of a comprehensive coaching model?
- Name two high-leverage actions that can be taken to activate this powerful strategy within the improvement process. Where would it be embedded? What metrics would be used to evaluate its impact?

CHAPTER SIX

STUDENTS ARE AT THE CENTER OF IT ALL

Leaders who are in pursuit of radical excellence take the stairs.

~ Kate

Radically excellent organizations value the interdependencies that catalyze improvement within and across the system. Moreover, leaders intentionally situate adults and implement practices that keep students at the center of all ambitious learning. Leaders at every level understand there are no short cuts and that improving outcomes for every student and having relentlessly high expectations of adults for students is their number one nonnegotiable. Instead of taking the elevator, relentlessly excellent leaders take the stairs, meaning they are committed to getting the conditions right, identifying the root of the root causes, and focusing on developing teachers so they can implement those powerful practices that can close gaps and grow students. Sure, taking an elevator is faster but the stairs provide a 360° view of what's behind, around the corner, and on the horizon. Put another way, districts that take the path of least resistance end up with the same results while districts who do the hard work understand that at the deepest levels, relentless improvement depends on the entire system working in synchrony.

THE EQUITY STAKE

Chapter 1 described the components of a highly effective improvement process that included a clearly articulated vision balanced with reality, and a set of tightly coordinated actions, measurements, common expectations, and practices dependent on shared accountability.

In Chapter 2, the landmark case of *Endrew F. v. Douglas Co. School District*, which ushered in a more substantive standard for ensuing students with disabilities were provided a free and appropriate public education (FAPE), was described.

It provided context for the legal and ethical considerations for ensuring students furthest away from opportunity were provided high-quality, ambitious instruction with their nondisabled, grade peers.

Chapter 3 described a system of support that was a responsive "nondirectional" framework for delivering rigorous, differentiated instruction and support inside the classroom. It described how collaborative teams were focused on identifying those effective practices that benefited every student, including students who needed additional, explicit, or more focused support to meet their academic and socioemotional/behavioral needs. The system supported the full continuum of students, including students learning English and students with disabilities.

Chapters 4 and 5 described how implementing a collaborative team structure and coaching model were two focused structures that should be a part of every improvement process. Implementing this type a comprehensive approach within the improvement process facilitated the delivery of ambitious instruction that improved outcomes for all students, and that also met the legal and ethical dimensions of special education. Students benefited and so did school districts because they could demonstrate meeting the *Endrew F.* standard, and for meeting the substantive obligation of providing a free and appropriate public education, the cornerstone of nearly all litigation. The imperative posed to the school improvement team was to claim the equity stake for the following questions:

1. Does anyone object to having educators design challenging lessons that are aligned to standards and that intentionally stretch students to their fullest potential?
2. Do principals want their teacher teams to use a variety of data to inform student progress so that real time course corrections can be made?

The answers to those questions, which were the same questions considered by the U.S. Supreme Court when it decided the *Endrew F.* case, drove the selection of high-leverage actions (Pareto Principle) aimed at ensuring students learned and achieved.

The next two chapters (6 and 7) will demonstrate how to embed the "higher standard" into the improvement process for students with disabilities. Each chapter will provide practical examples of effective practices, supports, and structures that not only meet the legal and ethical aspects of the special education law, but can also be applied to the full continuum of learners, including students at risk of failure, students learning English, and students with other complex needs. The Pareto Principle will illustrate how a few focused high-leverage actions, have the potential to radically improve student outcomes.

GETTING THE CONDITIONS RIGHT

Students with disabilities are first and foremost regular education students so when the conditions are right for all, students who are furthest away from opportunity, including students with disabilities can achieve. Figure 6.1 is a snapshot of the number of students served under the Individuals with Disabilities Education Act (IDEA, 2004) by category across the nation. A useful question to ask is how do these numbers compare to your state? Every district and school leader should visit the IDEA website (https://sites.ed.gov/idea/osep-fast-facts-school-aged-children-5-21-served-under-idea-part-b-21/) to compare how their state compares to the national average to gain a deeper understanding of who their students are and how they are achieving. What do the four categories with the highest number of students have in common? These disability categories, by definition, do not represent impairments that make achieving unattainable. For example, students identified with a specific learning disability, by definition, have average to above average intelligence but often have difficulty demonstrating their knowledge and understanding of the content. This is important because the trajectory of their lives could be negatively impacted by low expectations and a diminished education. But when school districts get the conditions right, students can grow, achieve, and graduate with a regular diploma. One of the telltale markers of school districts who value students with disabilities is their graduation rate. Graduating with a regular diploma is paramount to opening the door to a postsecondary education, apprenticeships, paid employment, and a meaningful life. It also legally ends the school district's obligations for providing a FAPE per the Individuals with Disabilities Education Act (2004). To highlight this point, the Massachusetts and Connecticut education departments recently revamped their Individual Education Program (IEP) forms and accompanying policies to amplify the voice of students' strengths, goals, and transition to life after school. That college and career focus can have direct links to well-paying jobs and for being contributing members of society. For example, businesses like Microsoft, Google, and other Route 128 industries have actively recruited graduates on the autism spectrum and other types of diverse learning styles precisely because of their inherent strengths. Their strong analytic skills, focus, perseverance, creative thinking, technical aptitude, and direct communication makes them highly sought after employees.

Figure 6.1 • *Number of students with disabilities, ages 5 (in Kindergarten) through 21, by disability category, served under IDEA, part B, in the US, outlying areas, and freely associated states: SY 2019–2020*

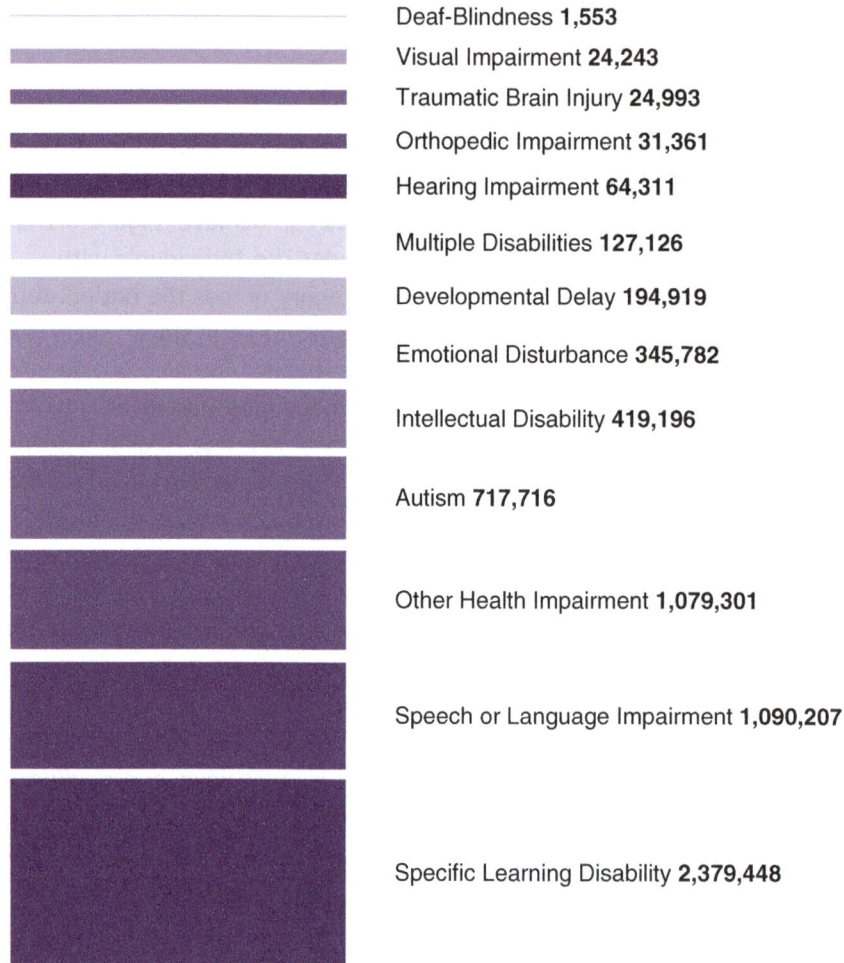

Deaf-Blindness **1,553**

Visual Impairment **24,243**

Traumatic Brain Injury **24,993**

Orthopedic Impairment **31,361**

Hearing Impairment **64,311**

Multiple Disabilities **127,126**

Developmental Delay **194,919**

Emotional Disturbance **345,782**

Intellectual Disability **419,196**

Autism **717,716**

Other Health Impairment **1,079,301**

Speech or Language Impairment **1,090,207**

Specific Learning Disability **2,379,448**

Source: U.S. Department of Education, EDFacts Data Warehouse (EDW). *IDEA Part B Child Count and Educational Environments Collection, 2019–2020.* https://www2.ed.gov/programs/osepidea/618-data/state-level-data-files/part-b-data/child-count-and-educational-environments/bchildcountandedenvironments2019-20.csv. All data for Wisconsin were suppressed due to data quality concerns. Data for Iowa was not available.

THE PRACTICES THAT BIND US

Now that the improvement team has gained a deeper understanding about the full continuum of its student body, it is time to put the comprehensive plan into motion. If the Double Helix serves as the foundational system of support, and coaching the connecting fiber, then efficacious instructional and behavioral practices serve as the arteries of radical excellence. Having a deeper understanding the *Endrew F.* Supreme Court decision, school districts can now shift from being satisfied by providing students with IEPs *a just more than trivial* education to a reengineered improvement process that explicitly accounts for the higher standard via shared accountability. To emphasize the reasons for this shift, look no further than the results from the *Rowley* standard on student achievement and graduation. According to the Office of Special Education Programs, 16.55% of students with disabilities dropped out of school, 72.6% graduated with a regular diploma, and 10.24% received an alternate certificate. Compare that to the 4.7% dropout rate for students without disabilities, and 86% of students graduating with a regular diploma. To reiterate what Chief Justice Roberts wrote in the *Endrew F.* decision, "a student offered an educational program providing 'merely more than *de minimis*' progress from year to year can hardly be said to have been offered an education at all. For children with disabilities, receiving instruction that aims so low would be tantamount to 'sitting idly ... awaiting the time when they were old enough to drop out.'"

The school district is now rightly positioned toward being radically excellent. It can be accomplished through the tightly aligned practices that bind the overall improvement process with the departments of Special Education, English Learner, and the other departments responsible for supporting students with complex needs. Implementing such an improvement process, with its dynamic system of support, embedded community of practice, instructional and leadership coaching, and the practices that are visible to everyone, can ensure relentless improvement throughout the entire organization. When these components are evident, the dimensions of the higher standard, including students' potential for growth, an IEP reasonably calculated to enable students to make progress in light of their circumstances, an IEP aligned to challenging standards, and a variety of data sources that are used to determine progress, and a FAPE can also be visible. That means the same measurements and data used to evaluate impact for students with IEPs would also be used to evaluate impact across the broader improvement process.

PUTTING IT INTO ACTION

Let's start with an IF/THEN proposition. If students with disabilities are to achieve, then special educators and related service providers must be situated with their regular education colleagues and valued as equal contributing members of the improvement process and the collaborative team structure.

The first step of implementation is by identifying how special education services are being provided. Examining where the majority of services are being delivered (i.e., the regular education classroom, the resource room, self-contained unit, therapy room) will inform what high-leverage shifts are needed. Examining the data collected from the *Students, Practices,* and *Resources* conditions of the Equity Audit will give the improvement team that needed information. For example, how many students with IEP are accessing advanced coursework, AP, or IB courses? What percentage of time are students with disabilities accessing grade-level content in their regular education classroom, which is their least restrictive environment (LRE), and meeting grade-level standards? A student's LRE is a legal requirement based on what the student needs to ambitiously address the gap created by their disability while meeting those challenging standards. Keeping in mind that special education is a service not a place, and that just sitting in a regular education classroom is insufficient for access and opportunity, is an important legal and ethical concept that often times shows up in peoples' beliefs and expectations about students with diverse needs. Even if an IEP states that a student is in the regular education classroom for 80% or more of their day, it does not necessarily equate to the quality of specially designed instruction and supports being provided. Thus, the improvement team will need to use the causal data from the root of the root analysis to determine if the newly identified practices and resource configurations will result in narrowing or eliminating the gaps caused by the disability. The evidence used should include the quality of the instruction and accompanying responsive supports, along with the analysis of student work and formative assessment data used by the collaboration teams. At its core, this analysis should be able to measure the impact of the practices for students with disabilities and, in turn, students overall.

The second step is by examining the quality of the IEPs according to the higher standard. The evidence to look for include written policies, procedures, guidelines, and templates (i.e., IEP forms) that explicitly describe how to incorporate the dimensions of the higher standard. The team members, which would include representation from the special education department, will need to determine if IEPs are reasonably calculated to enable students to make progress in light of their circumstances. A key concept is the "reasonable calculation." It represents the legal standard of one year's worth of growth during an academic year. To that end, IEPs will need to be aligned to challenging standards along with the variety of data sources will be used to determine the amount of progress made and whether students have received a free and appropriate public education or a FAPE.

The next step for ensuring students with disabilities are receiving ambitious instruction, which can also benefit all students, is by identifying those effective practices and supports that strategically address the students' academic or socioemotional/behavioral gap(s). It is especially important that teachers possess the necessary skills to codesign and codeliver aspects of specially designed instruction with precision because it builds shared accountability. It is also important that the majority of related services are delivered inside the classroom, so the skills can be generalized and transferred across environments. It also helps build the capacity of the regular educators so they can seamlessly support students when the special educators and not in the classroom. The team can use the data to make decisions about the substantive progress students have made per their IEP as well as use the data to measure progress of the overall improvement process.

BINDING PRACTICES THAT IMPACT LEARNING

Your school district or school may have a repository of practices that have proven to be effective. That's great so don't stop! Go deeper. Identify those instructional and socioemotional/behavioral practices that can impact learning for all students as well as meet the higher standard for students with IEPs. The more they are comprehensively implemented across the school, pursuant to the Double Helix, the more powerful the data will be for determining progress.

Let's start with a few strategic questions that can inform the measurements the school will use to evaluate their impact.

1. Are teachers engaging students in ways that makes them want to persist learning novel subject matter?
2. Are *all* the learning environments welcoming, supportive, and safe?
3. Do students have regular opportunities to learn from each other, collaborate, and build their metacognitive muscle through critical thinking?
4. Do students have regular opportunities to build their communication skills?
5. How are these skills being practiced across subjects and environments?

The answers to these questions will indicate the degree of deep learning that is taking place. The strategic practices can be most impactful when they are visible to teacher teams, coaches, support staff, related service providers, administrators, and, most importantly, students. The practices that help answer these questions can include direct instruction, differentiation, feedback, formative evaluation, and executive functioning. Identifying the strategic practices rather than the students allows for the right discussions by collaboration teams, coaching, and the IEP process.

The following sections of this chapter illustrate how to implement direct instruction, differentiation, feedback, formative evaluation, and executive functioning within the special education arena and how it can apply more broadly to students with other complex needs. The team is encouraged to think how these effective practices can apply more broadly to the school improvement process.

Let's begin with power of direct instruction.

DIRECT INSTRUCTION

The Individuals with Disabilities Education Act (IDEA, 2004) defines *direct instruction* as, "Specially designed instruction adapting, as appropriate to the needs of an eligible child, ... the content, methodology, or delivery of instruction to address the unique needs of the child that result from the child's disability; and to ensure access of the child to the general curriculum, so that the child can meet the educational standards within the jurisdiction of the public agency that apply to all children."

Putting this legal concept together with the effective practice of direct instruction can help meet the needs of the full continuum of students, inform the nondirectional Double Helix system of support, align to IEP goals, and be used to determine impact. Here are just some of the benefits of implementing direct instruction with the full continuum of students, including students with individual education programs (IEPs).

- IEP goals provide the basis for ambitious "direct" instruction (it's not a place).
- Discrete skills are taught via culturally relevant pedagogy, followed by discussion, feedback, and formative evaluation.
- Teachers can course-correct in real time via formative evaluation techniques.
- Metacognitive muscle is built so students can scaffold to their potential.
- Teachers use the data to assess progress toward goal attainment (FAPE).
- Teachers build their collective efficacy.
- Students improve because they know what the target is and are provided meaningful feedback.
- Reciprocal teaching is fostered.

Here is a an example of a lesson that incorporates direct instruction with an Ohio fourth-grade math standard for long division with remainders.

Introduction: Begin by activating prior knowledge. Ask students about their understanding of division and its connection to multiplication. Provide a brief overview of the lesson's goal of mastering long division with remainders.

Direct Instruction: Explicitly present the steps of long division using the whiteboard. Break down the process into manageable steps, ensuring each step is explained in a straightforward manner. Use visual aids and concrete examples to make the concept more accessible. Check for understanding.

Modeling: Demonstrate the long division process step by step. Emphasize the importance of organization and clear communication. Check for understanding after each step.

Scaffolded Instruction: Break the process into smaller parts and gradually build up to the full long division procedure.

Multisensory: Use manipulatives or tactile elements to support students with disabilities (i.e., counters to represent the dividend and divisor).

Guided Practice: Provide guided practice by solving a long division problem together as a class. Encourage students to ask questions and seek clarification during this process. Use the whiteboard for collaborative problem-solving, involving students in each step.

Differentiation: Tailor the support to individual needs. Some students may benefit from more visual cues, while others may require extra verbal explanations.

Independent Practice: Give one practice problem to students. Allow them to work independently, applying the skills they've learned. Circulate the room, provide assistance as needed, and observe students with disabilities to ensure their understanding. Intervene with direct instruction as needed.

Student Ownership: Have students share their solutions with the class (or tablemates). Encourage them to explain their thinking and the steps they took to arrive at the answers. This will promote student ownership of their learning, as each student becomes a teacher to their peers which reenforces concepts.

Feedback and Reflection: Provide constructive feedback on individual performance. Encourage students to reflect on their progress, identifying areas of success and potential areas for improvement. This metacognitive reflection fosters a sense of ownership and self-awareness.

Direct Instruction + Modeling + Practice = Student ownership of
their learning

DIFFERENTIATION

Differentiated instruction is a comprehensive and flexible process that includes the planning, preparation, and delivery of instruction to address the diversity of students' learning needs within the classroom. Utilizing this approach, teachers take into account who they teach, what they teach, where they teach, and how they teach. At its core, differentiated instruction focuses on the academic and social dimensions of learning and what the student needs in order to learn the content and demonstrate it across a variety of areas. Differentiated instruction focuses on the content, resources, and the product of learning. Implementing this approach is an effective instructional practice that benefits all students. Here are some of the benefits of implementing differentiated instruction for the full continuum of students, which includes students with IEPs.

> - Differentiating the *content*, *resources*, and *product* keeps students in the core and provides a consistent feedback loop about their learning.
> - Designing instruction to the edges is an intentional way to encourage student engagement, discovery, and empowerment.
> - Effective differentiation challenges students' expectations by involving them in setting goals with short-term targets and self-monitoring measures.

Differentiated instruction is a comprehensive, flexible, strength-based approach that meets the full continuum of students' learning needs within the classroom. When done within the collaborative team structure, teacher efficacy for the planning and delivery of ambitious instruction with stretch is developed, and the student product for evaluating their impact on learning is evident.

Here is an example of codesigning an eighth-grade lesson using the New Jersey standard of analyzing characters and their development in literature.

Teacher: Hi, I'm excited to sit down and plan our differentiated lesson for next week. It will be important that we tailor the instruction to meet the needs of the students with IEPs.

Special Education Teacher: Definitely. Differentiated instruction will be key. Let's start by discussing the diverse needs within our class, especially those outlined in

(Continued)

the IEPs. I've noticed some of our students require more visual aids, while others benefit from a multisensory approach.

Speech Language Pathologist: I agree. Some of our kiddos will need additional support decoding complex language structures and understanding figurative language. How about we break down the lesson into different layers, so we can account for the different ways they take in information?

Teacher: Great. First let's identify the core content we want all students to grasp. The New Jersey standard emphasizes character analysis, so we can start there. Then, we can create layers of support for different groups of our students.

Special Education Teacher: I suggest incorporating graphic organizers to help organize their thoughts and make character analysis more accessible. This will be great for our students acquiring English too.

Speech Language Pathologist: I can preteach the key vocabulary and provide sentence stems to help scaffold their responses. I can also work with small groups on specific language challenges related to the text.

Teacher: Great. Now, let's talk about how we'll assess their understanding. How can we make sure the lesson meets its objectives for all students?

Special Education Teacher: We should use formative assessments. This will allow us to adjust our strategies in real time. I can also create alternative assessments that focus on the same skill but does so in a way that the students can respond.

Speech Language Pathologist: We can also include oral responses as an alternative way for students to demonstrate their understanding, and aligns to the speaking and listening standards.

FEEDBACK

Here's a question everyone can relate to. How do you know if you're on the right track if you don't get any feedback? We use feedback all the time, whether it's a compass, GPS, Siri, or Alexa. The same reliance we have on immediate feedback also needs to be provided to students by their teachers. Feedback gives valuable information to students about their learning which is aligned to the success criteria for a unit of instruction. John Hattie (2023) emphasized that feedback should be focused so students can answer: "Where am I going? How am I going? And where to next?"

Another highly effective way of providing desired information to students is by using F.A.S.T. feedback. This method has been replicated across the country and it has improved the teaching and learning of countless educators. It works when the teacher provides the following feedback to students so they know how they are doing, what needs to improve, and how they can reach the destination of the learning target and success criteria. What is important to remember is that feedback needs to be clear, concise, and fair to the student. This method is also highly effective when used during the instructional coaching cycle.

F = Fair
A = Accurate
S = Specific
T = Timely

Here is an example of an essay rubric using a ninth-grade Georgia writing standard. Students are encouraged to reflect on their performance for each success criterion, providing insights into their understanding and efforts in the essay writing process. The feedback can be used formatively by both the teacher and the student and can also increase engagement and ownership of their learning. For this rubric, the student will assess their writing prior to turning in their draft for teacher feedback. The teacher can use their feedback with the draft and the rubric and provide the type of feedback that can lead to mastery. Some teachers use a recursive rubric or feedback cycle multiple times before the final submission occurs.

ESSAY FEEDBACK RUBRIC- NINTH-GRADE READING STANDARD

Another IF/THEN proposition might help put a fine point on the power of feedback. IF educators want to build the knowledge, skills, and metacognitive muscle for student growth so they are self-directed learners, THEN feedback that mutually benefits students, collaboration teams, IEP teams, and the improvement process is a powerful practice.

Essay feedback rubric – 9th grade reading standard (Georgia)

Criteria	Exemplary (4)	Proficient (3)	Basic (2)	Limited (1)	Student Input
Content & Analysis	The essay demonstrates a deep understanding of the topic, with a clear and compelling thesis statement. Ideas are well-developed, supported by relevant evidence, and critical thinking.	The essay presents a solid understanding of the topic, with a clear thesis statement. Ideas are developed and supported with relevant evidence. Critical thinking is evident.	The essay includes some relevant content but lacks depth and originality. Ideas may be underdeveloped or not consistently supported by evidence. Critical thinking is present but limited.	The essay lacks a clear thesis and may struggle to convey a coherent message. Ideas are unclear, and evidence is minimal or irrelevant. Critical thinking is lacking.	
Organization	The essay has a clear and logical structure, with a well-defined introduction, body paragraphs, and conclusion. Transitions are smooth, guiding the reader through the essay effectively.	The essay has a discernible structure, including an introduction, body paragraphs, and conclusion. Transitions are generally smooth, aiding in the flow of the essay.	The organization is somewhat unclear, with a basic introduction, body paragraphs, and conclusion. Transitions may be abrupt or lack clarity.	The essay lacks a clear organizational structure, making it challenging for the reader to follow the argument. Transitions are either absent or confusing.	
Language & Style	The essay exhibits a sophisticated and varied vocabulary, demonstrating a command of language. Sentences are	The essay exhibits a strong vocabulary, conveying ideas effectively. Sentences are generally well-constructed,	The language is basic and may lack variety. Some sentences are awkward or unclear, impacting the overall tone.	The language used is simplistic, with limited vocabulary. Sentences may be fragmented or confusing, detracting from the overall tone.	

(Continued)

(Continued)

Criteria	Exemplary (4)	Proficient (3)	Basic (2)	Limited (1)	Student Input
	well-crafted, varied, and enhance the overall tone.	contributing to an engaging tone.			
Grammar & Mechanics	The essay demonstrates a high level of proficiency in grammar, punctuation, and spelling. Essay has less than two errors and do not detract from the overall clarity of the writing.	The essay has three or less grammar, punctuation, and spelling errors, and any mistakes do not significantly impact the reader's understanding.	Essay has five or less grammar, punctuation, and spelling errors that affect clarity of writing and the reader's understanding.	The essay has more than five grammar, punctuation, and spelling errors, making it difficult to understand.	
Feedback & Revision	The student consistently engages with feedback, demonstrating a strong commitment to revising and improving their writing. Revisions show substantial growth and refinement.	The student generally incorporates feedback, making meaningful revisions to enhance their writing. Revisions contribute to improvement but may need further edits.	The student makes some attempt to address feedback, but revisions are limited or do not effectively improve the overall writing.	The student makes minimal or no effort to incorporate feedback, resulting in limited improvement and final writing.	

FORMATIVE EVALUATION

Like feedback, formative evaluation provides valuable precise information that can be used to make real-time decisions and course corrections. Relentless improvement depends on it. Collaboration teams should rely upon student work to discuss what's working, what's not, and what areas need to be adjusted. Formative evaluation can be quick and simple, but it's important that the quality of the input (i.e., exit ticket, student work sample) yields the desired output, so productive conversations can take place during the collaboration team meetings. Formative evaluation not only informs teachers of where their students are on the trajectory of mastery, it also provides the evidence of *their* impact on their students' learning. Teachers should ask themselves if what they are doing is positively impacting learning. What evidence will they use to evaluate whether students are meeting the success criteria for that lesson or unit? What strategies will they implement to ensure students learn the material? This reflective practice can be very effective for ensuring all students, including students with disabilities, have what they need to meet the objective or standard for that lesson. This practice has also been shown to increase student achievement across subjects.

Here are some examples of how a teacher can formatively assess student learning during a science class. All of these formative tools can be adapted for multiple subject, grades, and uses.

Formative Assessment

Exit Tickets:
Provide students with a brief question related to the day's lesson as they leave the class. This quick check-in helps the teacher assess their understanding and adjust instruction.

Concept Mapping:
Ask students to create a concept map to visually represent the connections between the different scientific concepts. This formative assessment allows the teacher to assess students' understanding of relationships within the topic.

Think-Pair-Share:
Have students individually think about a specific question or problem, discuss their thoughts with a partner, and then share their ideas with the class. This encourages collaboration and provides insight into individual and collective understanding. This allows the teacher to make adjusts to the instruction in real time.

(Continued)

(Continued)

One-Minute Papers:
Ask students to summarize the main concept or learning from the lesson in one minute. This quick reflection (written, oral, etc.) helps the teacher assess comprehension and allows students to reinforce their understanding. It can be adapted to a teacher-facilitated one-minute activity such as clickers, games, flip, poll, or other applications.

Gallery Walks:
Display diagrams, charts, or scientific models around the classroom. Have students rotate and discuss the information at each station. Each student leaves one sticky note identifying their main takeaway. This allows for peer-to-peer teaching, reinforcement of concepts, and provides the evidence needed so the teacher can adjust and correct any misunderstandings.

Modeling:
Students create a physical model or diagram to represent the scientific concept(s). This hands-on approach not only assesses their understanding but also taps into their creativity for multiple means of representation and expression.

EXECUTIVE FUNCTIONING

Humans are not born with expert executive skills and organizational strategies. They are taught, practiced, and refined with age and life experience. Yet for many students, the skills needed to plan, organize, demonstrate self-control and advocacy can be hard to acquire. Fortunately, the classroom environment can provide the perfect place for students to learn and practice in a judgment free environment. For students with diverse learning needs, including students at risk and students with disabilities, explicit instruction of executive functioning skills can be easily incorporated into lessons across content areas. For example, incorporating visual schedules with daily routines can help the student be ready for the next activity. This is especially helpful with transitions. Other examples include graphic organizers, self-monitoring checklists, socioemotional learning strategies, metacognitive reflections, and flexibility activities. Any or all should be explicitly taught first and then gradually released to the student. These skills often become the compensatory skills students lean on as they grow, mature, and matriculate through the grades. Building this metacognitive muscle is imperative to the ever-increasing complexity of learning. Teachers can scaffold skill development by planning for intentional practice, synthesizing multiple pieces of information, following step-by-step directions to solve mathematical problems, or using graphic organizers for written products.

The practices described in this chapter demonstrated the impact they can have on student growth, well-being, and achievement, and how each could be embedded within classroom instruction, and the broader school improvement process. Remembering that the IEP must be calculated to make at least one year's worth of growth, it makes sense to incorporate those practices that have similar effect sizes and impact. According to the research of John Hattie (2023) and others, a 0.40 effect size represents one year of growth over an academic year. So, the high-impact practices of explicit (direct) instruction which has an effect size of 0.63; feedback which has an effect size of 0.79; formative evaluation which has an effect size of 0.40; and executive functioning which has an effect size of 0.62, would be ambitious strategies for growing every student, regardless of language, disability, or other circumstance.

Now it is your turn. Reflect on the interconnectedness of the higher standard, effective practices, and the sources of data that can be used comprehensively to support to grow every student, while also meeting the legal and ethical standard for students with IEPs. These connections represent how schools can "take the stairs" so no one is left behind. When educators work collaboratively rather than in isolation, the beliefs about who is capable of learning can shift. Then nothing holds the improvement process back from achieving radical excellence.

Turning Ideas Into Action

- Ask this radical excellence question: If nothing were holding your school back from improving instructional practices, what actions need to be taken to develop all educators?
- Examine the results of the *Students*, *Practices*, and *Resources* conditions of the Equity Audit. How are special education services being provided? What is the evidence of impact? Where is the evidence of the higher standard visible? What evidence is being used to determine it?
- Are the practices that deliver the desired effect of at least one year's growth being implemented with fidelity across the continuum of students and specifically for students at risk and disabilities? If so, what is the evidence of the impact? If not, what actions are needed to ensure consistent and deep implementation?

(Continued)

(Continued)

- Are educators from all disciplines comprehensively situated to support students inside the classroom? Is it effective? What evidence is used to determine effectiveness? What steps need to be taken to strengthen shared accountability for ensuring the higher standard is being met?
- What interdependencies need to be documented within the improvement plan? Identify the metrics that will be used to evaluate the impact.
- How can resources be focused on the design features and shared accountability of the Double Helix? Identify the metrics that will be used to evaluate teacher and student impact.

CHAPTER SEVEN

AN IEP IS THE VEHICLE FOR FAPE

If a child can't learn the way we teach,
maybe we should teach the way they learn.

~ Ignacio Estrada

Chapter 6 described the effective practices that kept students at the center of it all. It provided the rationale and examples of how a few high-leveraged focused actions and practices can shift the improvement process from being a siloed one to a comprehensive one. This chapter will further describe how those same practices can substantively inform the higher standard and become visible for students with disabilities.

An individual education program (IEP) is *the* vehicle for demonstrating a free and appropriate public education, or FAPE. So, it is imperative that students with disabilities are acknowledged and provided the same ambitious education as their nondisabled peers so they can meet those challenging standards. While this has always been true, the Every Student Succeeds Act (2015) reinforced that fact. How it can become visible within the improvement process is by having relentlessly high expectations of the adults for students as the school district's #1 nonnegotiable. That expectation can, in turn, be manifested through the implementation of ambitious instruction with stretch. Meaning instruction which has been designed to the edges, including the intervening and enrichment strategies that guarantee ambitious learning for the full continuum of learners. Having that intentional design process provides for the elements of the higher standard to be intentionally embedded, aligned, and monitored. Students would be provided a *prospective* and *appropriately ambitious* IEP, that was *tailored* to meet the their unique needs, which was based on *data*. The higher standard could be achieved as well as the promise of ensuring ambitious instruction for all students.

To pull this thread even more, school districts would be better able to demonstrate their responsibility for meeting the substantive obligation of providing a free and appropriate public education (FAPE) because the same accountability measurements could be used to determine progress for all students. The integrated data system used for the school improvement process could also be used to determine a FAPE more effectively and efficiently. Utilizing such a robust data system would also have the potential to minimize litigation because it would allow for nimble and differentiated purposes.

What follows are examples of how educators can meet the higher standard while also benefiting the full continuum of learners with and without disabilities inside the classroom.

MEETING THE HIGHER STANDARD

Direct Instruction

The practice of direct instruction described in the previous chapter, can be comprehensively implemented to meet the higher, more substantive standard of improving outcomes for students with IEPs. Remember that the Individuals with Disabilities Education Act (IDEA, 2004) defines direct instruction as specially designed instruction, which can include adapting, as appropriate to the needs of an eligible child, "the content, methodology, or delivery of instruction to address the unique needs of the child that result from the child's disability; and to ensure access of the child to the general curriculum, so that the child can meet the educational standards within the jurisdiction of the public agency that apply to all children." That definition complements John Hattie's (2023) research on direct instruction, whereby educators explicitly teach a carefully sequenced curriculum, with built-in cumulative practice. Weaving both concepts together, direct instruction (explicit teaching), having an effect size of 0.63, or more than one year's worth of growth, would be a powerful instructional strategy and essential action of any school improvement plan. It is a powerful instructional practice that can also be used to meet the legal and ethical dimensions of special education.

This example illustrates how it can be comprehensively implemented with built in shared accountability. This comprehensive approach can foster the collective teacher efficacy by focusing on actionable data, addressing gaps, and scaffolding the rigor of instruction.

EXAMPLE

The teacher-based collaboration team agreed to implement direct instruction during reading instruction. An instructional coaching cycle was implemented to help build the skills of individual teacher(s), build the team's collective practice, and deepen the implementation of the data analysis used to determine progress.

This example illustrates of how a decoding and comprehension goal can be comprehensively delivered for a student with an IEP. This multifaceted approach can ensure the student's decoding and comprehension skill development. Progress can be effectively monitored using oral and written work samples. Finally, adjustments can be made in real time which will help meet the student's growth targets of their IEP.

EXAMPLE

Reading Goal: The student will receive direct reading instruction to increase decoding and comprehension using fifth-grade-level text. The special education teacher will collaborate with the fifth-grade language arts teacher to codesign and coserve, and will provide 70 minutes of direct instruction per week. The student will benefit from 125 minutes of codesigned reading activities targeting scaffolded decoding and comprehension strategies, 75 minutes of consultation across academic content areas, and 45 minutes of consultation by the speech language pathologist (SLP).

DIFFERENTIATION

Differentiated instruction is another powerful practice can be comprehensively implemented to meet the higher, more substantive standard of improving outcomes for students with IEPs. The following examples will demonstrate how this approach can be implemented across the curriculum for students with IEPs. Remember that differentiation focuses on the content, resources, and product while keeping students in the core and while providing students with a consistent feedback loop about their learning. Instruction is intentionally designed to the edges, which supports student engagement, discovery, and empowerment. Differentiated instruction effectively implemented, can strengthen student ownership of learning by being involved in goal-setting, identifying short-term growth targets and self-monitoring measures used to determine progress.

EXAMPLE

This example illustrates how educators from various disciplines can coplan and coserve a seventh-grade lesson on mathematical representation using the strategy of differentiated instruction.

The lesson is focused on analyzing proportional relationships and using them to solve real-world mathematical problems. Because the teachers regularly collaborate, they know their students strengths and areas of need and share accountability for student learning. For this lesson, students will be placed in groups and will rotate to different stations to solve the stated problem. Leveraging mathematical representation, students can choose how they will demonstrate their understanding of proportional relationships. Having smaller groups provide for the direct instruction of the skill, while setting students up for success so they can demonstrate the intended success criteria. In other words, the teachers meet their students where they are, scaffold learning, and pinpoint gaps in knowledge or misunderstanding and instruct with precision.

For students with IEPs having a written expression as a goal, they would have a choice of verbally, visually, or symbolically representing their answer. That's not to imply that written expression isn't important; it means for this aspect of the math lesson, the arduous task of written expression would be suspended so the student could focus on the cognitive skill needed to solve the problem. Increasing the cognitive load of written expression with mathematical representation of justifying one's reasoning, would be scaffolded after demonstrating mastery. Assessing the math skill versus the writing skill allows the teacher to accurately determine learning and make adjustments.

EXAMPLE

This example illustrates how a math goal can be comprehensively delivered for a student with an individual education program (IEP).

Math Goal: The student will independently demonstrate proficiency in sequential problem-solving and expression skills, as measured by successfully identifying and applying the steps for solving grade-level equations in alignment with seventh-grade math standards.

The special education teacher will collaborate with the seventh-grade math teacher, SLP, and OT for 50 minutes per week to codesign instruction using differentiated strategies for content, resources, and product. The student will receive 60 minutes of explicit instruction per week to analyze and apply mathematical representation for solving grade-level equations (i.e., proportional relationships). Progress will be monitored through both formative and summative evaluations.

The speech-language pathologist (SLP) will provide 30 minutes of consultation services per week to support the student's executive functioning, as well as expressive and receptive language strategies. These strategies will be integrated into math instruction to enhance the student's overall problem-solving and communication skills.

The occupational therapist (OT) will provide 20 minutes of consultation services per week to address fine motor and attention-to-task strategies. These strategies will be embedded into the math instruction to support the student's ability to apply sequential problem-solving.

EVERY BEHAVIOR HAS A PURPOSE

The final example illustrates how effective behavioral practices can meet the needs students with IEPs as well as support the overall social and emotional development of all students. Acknowledging that all behavior has a purpose whether it is outwardly disruptive or internally protective will inform the proactive strategies that are implemented individually or collectively. For example, on-task or off-task behaviors can impede access to rigorous and relevant content. For students with IEPs, disruptive behaviors can be used as an inaccurate justification for a more restrictive environment. Think back to Part B Child Count by Disability (Figure 6.1) and the number of students identified with an Emotional Disability label. That label can equate to a very restrictive environment with little to no peer modeling. Furthermore, such an environment often times has diminished academic rigor. Yet, for other students, behaviors such as shyness, compliance, and being withdrawn can mask issues related to engagement, persistence, and potential.

To address these areas of development, a comprehensive approach delivered with precision is needed. Effective comprehensive behavioral intervention practices involve the collaboration and shared accountability across disciplines (regular and special education teacher, related services, specials), and the student. A proactive approach involves culturally and linguistically engaging lessons. Explicit academic and socioemotional instruction is practiced across content areas to scaffold the metacognitive muscle of persistence and executive functioning. Common expectations, routines, and standards are established and adhered, student voice is valued and supported and development, and a healthy school climate and culture is promoted. Finally, direct instruction is deeply implemented and scaffolded. Systematically implementing effective behavioral strategies can result in tangible growth and achievement, and positive movement for students' least restrictive environment (LRE).

These examples illustrate how implementing proactive, consistent behavioral supports with explicit instruction can result in tangible improvement for students with IEPs and for demonstrating a free and appropriate public education.

> - Reeducation in disruptive behaviors that result in fewer office referrals and disciplinary actions
> - Improved academic engagement as measured by reduced absenteeism, work completion, and agency for one's learning
> - Decrease number of students with IEPs in restrictive settings as measured by improved LRE data
> - Reflective student feedback as measured by positive feelings of belonging and self-advocacy using surveys, observations, and conferencing

A Comprehensive Eye Means a Comprehensive Approach

School districts across the nation have been called upon to ameliorate the learning loss and stunted behavioral development of the pandemic. The examples provided in this chapter offer clear and comprehensive ways of achieving that call and for meeting the higher standard and a FAPE for students with disabilities. But no one person or discipline can do it alone. It will take the collective power of the school improvement process to commit to deeply implementing a set of focused, high-leverage practices and structures and then monitoring them for their intended impact.

Now it is your turn. Think how the examples presented in this chapter have the potential to disrupt a current fragmented and siloed system. Think what it would take to implement such a comprehensive approach at its deepest levels. Examine how the federal rescue money that was meant to ameliorate academic and socioemotional/behavioral learning loss has been prioritized by your district. Think about the sustainable professional practices that are needed to build an accountability system that is cohesive, intentional, and shared by all educators. Reflecting on these will result in the opportunity to relentlessly pursue excellence while also meeting the legal and ethical dimensions of what a free and appropriate public education means for students with disabilities.

Turning Ideas Into Action

- Ask this radical excellence question: If nothing were holding your school back from improving the quality of special education services, how would they be improved? What would need to change? Challenge the team to identify the strategies that would be most effective.
- What structural changes would need to be in place? Think about district-level policies, procedures, eligibility criteria, data systems, IEP software programs.
- What adult learning and supports would need be provided and supported? What evidence would be used to determine the impact of those actions?
- Does the district have robust and integrated data systems that are used to make accurate decisions about the trajectory of student growth? If not, what would be needed? Be specific.
- How can resources be directed to support this comprehensive approach?

CHAPTER EIGHT

ALIGNMENT IS A FORCE MULTIPLIER

The five separate fingers are five independent units.
Close them and the fist multiplies strength.
This is organization.

~ James Cash Penney

Whether it's automation, behavioral change, or an attitude adjustment, small changes can have a profound effect. That's the idea behind the concept of a force multiplier. For example, automating simple things like grouping sender emails can result in greater efficiency for sending responses and more time focusing on what's important. Having walking meetings can result in improved blood pressure or BMI. Or shifting one's attitude away from critical self-talk to determined optimism, can result in manifesting the steps needed to achieve one's goals. To emphasize this point relative to education, implementing force multiplying practices aimed at improving student outcomes can result in dramatic improvements across the entire organization.

You might be saying this all sounds right but how does our team go about aligning all these disparate parts? Just like Mr. Penney illustrated, each finger is independent of the other but when they are brought together for a common purpose, their strength is multiplied.

ALIGNMENT IS THE FORCE MULTIPLIER

A highly effective improvement process described in the first chapter depends on a tightly unified organization. The overarching district-level process [plan] would cascade to an aligned school improvement plan along with a set of common expectations and collaborative structures so that those identified high-leverage professional practices can be deeply implemented including inside classroom. Then, shared accountability and interdependencies would be explicitly aligned within and across the organization. Having a unified district can that flows into the school plan provides the force multiplier levers of transformation.

The *Resources* and *Governance* data of the Equity Audit provide the contours for this unified alignment by identifying the *force multiplying* structures and ways of doing business that can support the improvement efforts. The *Resources* condition assesses the human, fiscal, and material resources meant to support students. Whereas the *Governance* condition assesses alignment of the structures within and across and the organization and the larger community.

Aligned Resources

Radical excellence can only happen when all the resources are focused on the levers for improvement. Now is the time to stand up the teams' nonnegotiable of high expectations of the adults for their students. If the improvement process has all the elements described in the previous chapters, then the human, fiscal, and material resources can comprehensively support the goals and measurements used to evaluate impact of student growth. Don't stop—go deeper to make the interdependent connections resilient within each department and across the district as a whole. Alignment is straightforward but it will require the commitment of everyone throughout the organization, including the board of education to make it a dynamic process. Here are a few suggested steps to comprehensively align all the strands.

The first step of alignment is to look through the lens of what students need within each school. Who are the most impactful teachers, related providers, and principals? Are they at schools with the least or most need? If nothing were holding the team back, where would the most effective educators be assigned? Comprehensively situating the adults will be the key to sustained improvement.

The second step is to identify the types of professional development and adult learning needed to comprehensively instruct the academic and social emotional dimensions of learning of the full continuum students in each building. Purposefully collaborate with the departments within the district or externally to meet those needs. For example, the Teaching & Learning, Special Education, and English Learner departments could collaborate to codesign and lead a schoolwide institutes on how to embed universal design across grades or across content areas. This collaborative structure would include the identified funds that could be combined or braided to support the training and the coaching support needed for deep implementation. The department leaders could meet with the business office to align the funds with the actions, indicators, and metrics of the goals of the improvement process and in accordance with all regulations. Finally, the actions of interdependent accountability would be documented in an efficient and effective manner.

The next step of alignment is engaging the IT department. They are expert in thinking through processes so lean on them to be an integral part of the solution. The leaders of the department would meet with the other departments to find the synchronies and gaps for integrating the a robust data system, including the system of support, health, accommodation, language, and the IEP software programs. The goal would be the same data that is used for everyone would also be used with students with the full continuum of complex needs. The data would help inform instruction, assessment, intervention, enrichment, and growth toward academic and socioemotional achievement. All data would be accessible throughout, which in turn, would inform the high-leverage improvement actions.

Then, all materials would be aligned to support the improvement actions. Focus only on those materials that can support and improve practices inside the classroom. This is where the team can leverage its authority to interrupt the "razzle dazzle" from vendors with their sophisticated algorithms, software programs, and slick presentations promising to increase student scores. Instead, the improvement process will be laser focused on building the knowledge, skills, and dispositions of the adults so that ambitious learning can occur, regardless of where students sit on the continuum of learning.

Finally, it will be important to establish the cadence for adult learning on topics of financial, data, and legal literacy. This aligned support can benefit principals, administrators at all levels, teachers, students, and families. This force multiplier of aligned resources can then rightly situate the school improvement work and build shared accountability by keeping a relentless focus on what matters!

To illustrate how aligned resources can focus the improvement process, the Waytogo School District will be used as an example. The district strategically assessed and aligned their resources to meet the diverse needs of its students, foster an environment for shared accountability, and supported the pathways for academic success.

Human Resources: The district conducted a comprehensive evaluation of existing staff, their roles, and expertise. They surveyed staff to identify skills, strengths, and areas for professional development. Next, they analyzed teacher–student ratios to ensure optimal classroom support, including specialized staff such as counselors, special education teachers, language specialists, social workers, physical and occupational therapists based on student requirements. The team identified professional development and instructional coaching, to support the growth professional practices of its educators.

Fiscal Resources: The district evaluated the budget allocation process of the school district. They reviewed how funds were distributed, specifically focusing on student-centric programs and strategies detailed in the improvement process. They analyzed spending patterns to prioritize allocations based on student needs for each school.

Material Resources: The district assessed the adequacy and effectiveness of instructional materials, technology, and facilities. They inventoried textbooks, materials, and technology resources and connectivity in each school. They identify gaps in technology access for students and identified solutions.

Aligned Governance

The final connection of the radical excellence improvement process is having an aligned governance structure. This structure encompasses the alignment of board of education, district, school, and teacher collaborative teams so that everyone and every recourse is focused on what matters—improved outcomes for students by way of the adult practices. This aligned continuous cycle cascades to each level of leadership team which in turn, informs the adoption of district policies support the work.

The role of the board then, is an integral force multiplier because the structure provides the contours for the collective decisions and accountability. Among the boards many important responsibilities, is being the collective voice for explaining the WHY of education. To meet this awesome responsibility, board members can take ownership of the policies that support the improvement efforts of the district. In order to be the most effective in their role, board members will need data presented in user-friendly ways, so they can make sense of it, and be able to ask deep questions that illicit connected responses. Then they will be better able to communicate the rationale for their proposed actions, and advocate for the levers of improvement to the community. But board members can only make the case if they possess a differentiated view of each school. Moreover, members must feel safe to challenge assumptions, expectations, and biases about what students "can't do" in order to empower the district to implement the practices that can transform the system into a dynamic organization. The best way to accomplish this through positive and trusting professional relationships with leadership, educators, students, and families, and the community. When these comprehensive structures are valued and the policies and practices that support improvement becomes *the* way of doing business, then every student can grow, thrive, and achieve.

Looking back at the concentric circles (Figure 4.1) in Chapter 4, the tight alignment at the district, school, and teacher team levels serve as the force multiplier for shared accountability and relentless improvement. The interdependencies provide the contours for executing on improvement goals, coupled with the practices and systems that support the growth every student.

Let's use the Waytogo School District again to illustrate how to align governance. The board wanted to strengthen its governance structure, enhance collaboration between the board and the leadership team, and improve engagement with the community to better serve the needs of students and families.

Governance Structure: The board wanted to make sure the governing structures aligned and supported the mission of the district. They engaged in a review bylaws, policies, procedures, and committee structures to determine their effectiveness for addressing district priorities. The board identified redundancies and gaps that inhibited the efficient decision-making process, and created procedures that were aimed at increasing clarity and transparency.

Board of Education and Leadership Team: The board wanted to enhance collaboration and build trust between them and districtwide leadership. The board reviewed their roles, responsibilities, and decision-making processes to make sure there were clear channels for communication and collaboration. Together they aligned the strategic priorities of the board with the district improvement process. The board and leadership team identified professional development and training that would be mutually beneficial to better support schools, families, and the community.

Community Engagement: The board and leadership team examined how they currently engaged with families and the community. The analysis revealed opportunities to improve participation in the decision-making process through advisory groups and community forums. The team also identified multiple ways for effectively communicating the priorities of the district, and established a calendar for providing updates to the community about decisions, and districtwide improvement.

Now it's your turn. Keep students at the center as the team thinks through the force multipliers of the improvement plan. Then consider the questions for turning ideas into actions.

Turning Ideas Into Action

- Ask this radical excellence question: If nothing were holding your team back from aligning resources and governance structures, how would the district go about it? Name the steps, the interdependencies of the departments, and the focused, aligned actions. Be specific.
- How would the improvement team and board communicate the WHY for the alignment? What barriers might there be and what specific supports would be needed to overcome them? Be specific.
- What protocols would be used to help build the interdependent structures that align to the improvement process? Be specific.
- Name two high-leverage actions the team can take to address the identified alignment gaps. Commit to taking the needed steps to improve alignment within and across the district.

CHAPTER NINE

BE THE FLOW

Don't go with the flow,
be the flow.

~ Jay Z

This is it. The moment has arrived to stand up all the hard work the team has done to radically improve outcomes for every student. You've disrupted the paper tiger of shallow, nibble-around-the-edges products that vendors try to razzle-dazzle schools into buying. No, your team realized that the power resides within, and the members have committed to aligning every effort, practice, and resource what will dismantle a fragmented system so that a compressive system of relentless improvement can be realized. Bravo! Spend five minutes celebrating this accomplishment. Now turn to the essential interdependent work of monitoring and adjusting the school improvement plan. To paraphrase what Ben Franklin said in Chapter 1, without continual growth and progress, improvement and success have no meaning. To that end, monitoring the effectiveness of the actions is paramount so adjustments can be made, and excellence achieved. Keep your eye on what matters most—students.

This book started with the broad concepts of designing a radically excellent improvement process that included every student. Then, we went deeper into the landmark Supreme Court decision that shifted the floor of special education. Then we went very deep into the practices that benefit all and specifically for students with complex needs including special education. The symbiotic relationship between and among the practices provided the pathway for collective efficacy and shared accountability. Then, we pulled back up and out again to show how this comprehensive system can bring alignment and sanity to the overall improvement process. Now, we are at the threshold of excellence. Now it is time to be the flow.

BE THE FLOW

At the time of this writing, the scores from the National Assessment of Education Progress (NAEP, 2023) were just published. They showed the average understanding of math and reading for thirteen-year-olds plummeted by levels not seen since the 1990s and 1970s, respectively. The results are even more pronounced for other groups of students with complex needs, including students with disabilities (Figure 9.1). While it may be convenient to attribute the learning loss to the pandemic, it needs to be acknowledged that fragmentation and insufficiently ambitious practices have also contributed to the decline. To get to the root of the root, your improvement team decided to interrupt the tinkering that has been in place and implemented a comprehensively aligned process that situates students at the center of it all. This commitment is the very definition of being the flow!

Figure 9.1 • *Decline since the pandemic*

	Since pandemic 2020-2023	Prior to pandemic 2012-2020
Race/ethnicity	↓ All race/ethnicities except Asian	↓ Black, Hispanic
Gender	↓ Male, Female	↓ Male, Female
Economically disadvantaged status	↓ Both economically disadvantaged and not	↓ Economically disadvantaged
Region	↓ All regions	↓ Northeast, South
School location	↓ All locations	↓ City, Suburban
Status as students with disabilities	↓ Both students with disabilities and not	↓ Both students with disabilities and not
Status as English Learners	↓ Both English learners and not	↓ Both English learners and not

↓ Score decrease

Note: results are not available for American Indian/Alaska Native students in 2012

Source: National Assessment of Educational Progress (2023).

Engaging in a continuous cycle of monitoring and adjusting are two powerful ways of being the flow. The process involves intentionally asking if the high-leverage actions that are being delivered with precision are having the intended impact, and if so, what evidence is being used to determine that impact. This question is critical because students succeed as a result of actions taken by the adults. Therefore, engaging in regular cycles of data analysis throughout the quarter, trimester, semester, and academic year can help the teams at all levels of the organization determine the rate of progress, growth, and achievement.

BE THE FLOW AND THE FORCE MULTIPLIER

Another way your improvement process can be the flow is by being relentlessly aligned with the professional practices, the coaching framework, and the collaborative team structure that reside within the system of support. The Double Helix rightly values an interdependent alignment over a fragmented system that for many states and school districts is on a collision course with the seismic funding cliff coming September 2024. Marguerite Roza (Roza & Silberstein, 2023) at the Edunomics Lab, who is the premier authority on school finance, predicts that districts that use the recovery funds for recurring obligations such as backfilling budgets, hiring new teachers and staff, or paying for permanent raises are most at risk when the funding stops. Other risk factors that involve districts of all sizes and types include those with declining enrollments, offering large raises that exceed the typical range of 1% to 2%, and districts that are dependent of state revenues, especially if the states have been hit by economic downturns.

The antidote to these realities is an aligned system of support that is embedded within the overall improvement process because it focuses on how the adults within each department work together on behalf of the student. Principals, teachers, related service providers, staff, students, and families know what is being monitored, so that key adjustments can be made in accordance with the improvement plan—nothing else. Put another way, relentless focus + alignment = radical improvement. Not just for some but for everyone.

CONCLUSION

The comment Chief Justice Roberts wrote, "When all is said and done, a student offered an educational program providing 'merely more than *de minimis*' progress from year to year can hardly be said to have been offered an education at all," holds true for all students, especially in light of the cavernous learning losses that exist today. For students with disabilities and other disengaged students, the notion of "aiming so low" that it is tantamount to "sitting idly by" waiting for them to simply drop out must be courageously disrupted at every level of the educational organization.

The improvement team now possesses the tools to disrupt deficit thinking and design a strength-based improvement process that situates students at the center and with adults comprehensively situated to support with precision. When the process is fully implemented, it will be like breathing. Inhale the components of the equity audit and exhale the powerful aligned practices that show impact. Inhale the Double Helix System of Support and exhale those high-effect strategies that attack gaps and reduce the number of students inappropriately identified as failures, at risk, and disabled. Finally, deeply inhale the dimensions of the *Endrew F.* higher standard and exhale a free and appropriate public education in the students' least restrictive environment that positively changes the trajectory from sitting idle to becoming a valuable, contributing member of society.

If not now, when? If not you, who?
Be the flow because students need you!

APPENDIX A: EQUITY AUDIT DESCRIPTION

THE FIVE CONDITIONS

The purpose of the Equity Audit is to examine the level of implementation across the five conditions for creating a comprehensive improvement process. The five conditions for creating a comprehensive, equity-focused process include the following:

1. General and Social Characteristics
   The purpose of this condition is to understand the organization as a whole. It provides a meaningful way to understand the context. It provides a connected understanding of who the students are and the educators who are responsible for ensuring learning.

2. Students
   The purpose is to measure the conditions under which students have access to high-quality educational and socioemotional instruction and supports. It examines the degree to which a high-quality, rigorous curriculum and a system of support are implemented within the classroom and across disciplines.

3. Practices
   The purpose of this condition is to understand the adult competencies related to the practices of teaching and learning, as well as socioemotional, cultural, and linguistic competencies to address opportunity gaps. It identifies the effective practices that benefit all students, including students with disabilities.

4. Resources
   The purpose of this condition is to assess the human, fiscal, and material resources that support students, families, teachers, school, and district. It assesses the degree of aligned resources across and within the district and school(s).

5. Governance
   The purpose of this condition is to determine the alignment of governance across and within the system that support the development of teacher, principal, and district leadership.

APPENDIX B: EQUITY AUDIT

EXAMINING THE FIVE CONDITIONS FOR CREATING A HOLISTIC SYSTEM

The Big Picture: General and Social Characteristics

The purpose of this condition is to understand the district as a whole. It is a meaningful way to understand the context.

Condition	Evidence
Number of students enrolled – District	
Number of students enrolled – School(s)	
SUBGROUP (percent of total)	
Gifted	
Disability	
At-risk	
Economically Disadvantaged	
English Learner	
Foster	

(Continued)

(Continued)

Homeless	
Military	
Any other "label"	

RACE/ETHNICITY (percent of total)	
White	
African American	
Hispanic	
Asian	
More than two races	
Amy other self-identification	

TEACHING STAFF	
Total by district and school	
Years of service	
Level of education	
Race/Ethnicity (representative of the students in the community/district/school)	Yes _____ No _____
Gender	Male _____ Female _____ Other _____

DISCIPLINE DATA	
District	
By School	

By Subgroup	
By Race/Ethnicity	

ACHIEVEMENT DATA	
District	
School	
Subgroups	

FINANCE	
District: Per Pupil	
School: Per Pupil	

Students

The purpose is to measure the conditions under which students have access to high-quality educational, social emotional instruction, and systems of support.

Percent of students accessing advanced or IB course(s)	
Percent of students with disabilities accessing advanced or IB course(s)	
Percent of girls accessing advanced or IB course(s)	
Percent of boys of accessing advanced or IB course(s)	
Percent of African American (AA) and Hispanic (H) students accessing advanced or IB course(s)	AA _____ H _____

(Continued)

(Continued)

Percent of time students with disabilities are accessing grade level content in the regular education classroom (Least Restrictive Environment)	
Students placed out of district - by subgroup and/or disability	

SYSTEM OF SUPPORT

Has a written philosophy and framework	
Has written policies describing a preventative system of support (SoS)	
Has a written description for monitoring the degree of implementation	
Clearly written description for <u>how</u> students proactively receive supports	
Clearly written description for <u>when</u> students receive supports (decision points)	
Clear decision-making procedures/ protocols in place	
Clear cycles of data review in place	

DISCIPLINE

Total number of Suspension & Expulsions	
Percent of Suspensions – by subgroup	
Percent of Expulsions – by subgroup	

Practices

The purpose of this condition is to understand the adult competencies related to the teaching & learning, social, emotional, cultural, and linguistic practices for addressing opportunity gaps (district/school).

General Education: Do ALL students receive high quality grade level education (indicators)	
High expectations for learning (indicators)	
Prevention: System of Support	
Process: Rules of engagement for the SoS	
IDEA Eligibility Process	
UDL and Assistive Technology	
Social Emotional Learning (SEL)	
Assessment used to inform instruction and supports (how and why)	
Data Literacy	

Resources

The purpose of this condition is to assess the human, fiscal, material resources that support the students, families, teachers, school, and district.

Human	
Representative teaching and support staff (including EL)	
Culturally Responsive Practices (CRP)	
Principals are data literate	
Principals are financial literate	
Principals are legal literate	
Assignment of new and tenured staff	
Fiscal/Budgets	

(Continued)

(Continued)	
The district use student-based budgeting	
Per Pupil Expenditure	
Materials/Resources (UDL)	
Technology	
Integrated data systems	
Culturally relevant materials	

Governance

The purpose of this condition is to determine the alignment of governance across and within the system.

Board of Education	
District Policies	
District Leadership Team	
Building Leadership Team	
Teacher Leadership Team	
Other Collaborative Team Structure(s)	

APPENDIX C: EQUITY AUDIT GUIDING QUESTIONS

GUIDING QUESTIONS

For each of the *5 Conditions* you will address a set of Guiding Questions below. Your response to these questions will inform the high leverage actions taken to advance the academic and nonacademic outcomes for every student.

Guiding Questions for Condition 1: The Context

1. What does the data show?
2. What could be the causes from the data?
3. What could be structural antecedents of the causal data?
4. Do the adults in the building reflect the students and the community?
5. What are two high-leverage actions the district or school can take to address the structural inequities?

Guiding Questions for Condition 2: The Students

1. What does the data show?
2. What could be the causes from the data?
3. What could be structural antecedents of the causal data?
4. What are two high-leverage actions the district or school can take to address the structural inequities?

Guiding Questions for Condition 3: The Practices

1. What does the data show?
2. What could be the causes from the data?
3. What could be structural antecedents of the causal data?
4. Do the practices reflect an asset-based, culturally, and linguistically responsive approach to teaching and learning?
5. What are two high-leverage actions the district or school can take to address the structural inequities?

Guiding Questions for Condition 4: The Resources

1. What does the data show?
2. What could be the causes from the data?
3. What could be structural antecedents of the causal data?
4. What are two high-leverage actions the district or school can take to bring alignment?

Guiding Questions for Condition 5: The Governance

1. What does the data show?
2. What could be the causes from the data?
3. What could be structural antecedents of the causal data?
4. What are two high-leverage actions the district or school can take to bring alignment across the organization?

APPENDIX D: SAMPLE SECTIONS OF AN EQUITY AUDIT

CONDITION ONE: GENERAL AND SOCIAL CHARACTERISTICS

Yourtown Metropolitan School District

Number of students enrolled—district	35,250
Number of students enrolled—school	Completed per school
SUBGROUP (percentage of total)	
Gifted	8%
Disability	19%
At-risk	43%
Economically Disadvantaged	97%
English Learner	13%
Foster	2%
Homeless	6%
Military	0%
Any other "label"	
RACE/ETHNICITY (percentage of total)	
White	14.5%
African American	63.8%
Hispanic	17.2%
Asian	1.3%
More than two races	2.8%

(Continued)

(Continued)	
ANY other self-identification	0.2%
TEACHING STAFF	
Total by district and school	District: 14 years
Years of service	District: Male 14.4 Years Female 15.3 years
Level of education	Male: (99.3% bachelors) (62% masters)
	Female: (99.1% bachelors) (67.3% masters)

Race/Ethnicity (representative of the students in the community/district/school)	Yes ____ No _X_
Gender	Male 18,031 Female 16,859
DISCIPLINE DATA	
District	Emergency removal by district personnel Out of school suspensions 12,448 In school suspensions 578 Expulsion <10
By School	Complete per school
By Subgroup	Students with Disabilities District: Disruptive behavior 1,187 Fighting 1,233 Harassment 297 Theft 36 Truancy 177
By Race/Ethnicity	Out of School Suspensions: Black 35

	Hispanic 12
	White 11
	Fighting:
	Black 29
	Hispanic <10
	White <10
	Harassment:
	Black 20
	Hispanic <10
	White <10
ACHIEVEMENT DATA	
District	50.5%
School	Complete per school
Subgroups	23%
FINANCE	
District: Per Pupil	$20,521
School: Per Pupil	Complete per school

1. What does the data show? The data shows that Yourtown Metropolitan Schools has a predominantly African American student body, who, when compared to other districts in the state, is large. The district achievement is very low and needs to be addressed immediately. The number of years that teachers have taught is average compared to other districts around the region.

2. What could be the causes from the data? Yourtown School District resides within a large community that has lost its manufacturing base. Families have stayed but there are lack economic opportunities. Discipline data for students with disabilities is high compared to other groups. The lack of a representative teaching staff could be an issue but could also be the result of

the lack of cultural competencies and resources to increase engagement. Deeper analysis is needed.

3. What could be structural antecedents of the causal data? Longstanding disinvestment of the community which includes job opportunities, food deserts, and lack of social safety networks. Lack of culturally responsive pedagogy and resources to increase student engagement.

4. Do the adults in the district reflect the students and the community? Unfortunately, the teaching staff does not reflect the students we serve. The majority of the adults are white women and only a handful of men regardless of race or ethnicity.

5. What are two high-leverage actions the district (or school) can take to address the structural inequities?

Two high-leverage leadership actions include collaborating with the human resources department to develop marketing materials that attract a more diverse pool of candidates. Along with that, would be developing interview questions that would help the district identify biases of candidates to make sure they have high expectations for students.

CONDITION TWO: STUDENTS

Sample response to one of the guiding questions: What does the data show?

Two areas of concern emerged from the data. The first is related to discipline. The second is related to accessing rigorous learning opportunities.

Discipline: While the total number of suspensions within the district was low (40 suspensions), students with disabilities made up nearly half of the incidents (19). Black students were suspended at a rate of 7.3% of the total population of Black students within the district. White students were suspended at a rate of only 1.1% of the total population within the demographic group. More students were suspended at the middle and high school levels.

In terms of equitable learning opportunities, the data shows that only 0.9% of students with disabilities, 2% of African Americans students, and 9% of Hispanic students take advanced placement (AP) courses across the district, compared to 39% of the total population accessing AP courses. The district has a multitiered system of support at Tiers 2 and 3, but achievement within advanced courses is not equitable and achievement is inconsistent. Also, students in these tiers stay in them for multiple years which suggests it is ineffective.

CONDITION THREE: PRACTICES

ABC School

General Education: Do **ALL** students receive high-quality grade-level education? (Indicators)	The data shows that all students are **not** receiving a high-quality grade-level education at my school.
	Students without disabilities: Over the past few years, our district has made attempts to provide a high-quality grade-level education to students without disabilities.
	Students with disabilities: The data/evidence shows our building is not providing a high-quality grade-level education to our students with disabilities, mainly because these students aren't being held to the same standards as their typically developing peers. Students with disabilities are not really considered when the building goals are created. Additionally, students' Alternate Assessment scores are not a part of any district or school review. The SPED administration isn't asked or doesn't see if/how better instruction can be provided. Many students with IEPs don't participate in school assessments throughout the year (i.e., MAP, DIBEL, other). Special ed teachers don't have access to grade-level math content that is modified to meet our students' needs. Another major issue is there is no overarching expectations from the SPED department to ensure teachers are providing a high-quality education to students. Many SPED teachers are providing services to their students and have individual data that shows the student progress on their goals. But there is no districtwide expectation or vision to show how teachers can provide high-quality instruction to students with disabilities.

(Continued)

〈 **97** 〉

(Continued)

High expectations for learning (Indicators)	I can't point to any evidence that shows how high expectations for learning are set for all students.
	Students without disabilities: Many of the programs and examples I've listed above show that high expectations are set for students without disabilities. For example, these students are expected to progress through a year's worth of math lessons through the curriculum. We use student MAP scores in the fall, and expect each students' MAPs score to improve over the year. Also, our Building Leadership Team (BLT) can set high expectations for student learning based on the students' state tests results from the previous year. Finally, through teacher evaluations, administrators can also ensure that high expectations are set for students.
	Students with disabilities: I couldn't find evidence that shows our school has officially set high expectations for students with disabilities. The SPED teachers set high expectations for students, but there's no districtwide expectation. Administration does not check to see what expectations are being set for students with IEPs, or what kind of progress they are making on the expectations the SPED teachers set. My principal doesn't usually ask to see student data and how it's been monitored throughout the year on the goals or expectations.
Prevention: System of Support (SoS)	The school just started implementing academic- and behavioral-tiered supports, but each area and each tier is discrete (stand-alone) with no connection to the improvement process.

SoS Process: Rules of Engagement	Processes for moving through the system of support hasn't been developed yet.
IDEA Eligibility Process	Our district does not have a written system to ensure that interventions are taking place first before a special education referral is considered. There's an expectation that intervention takes place first, but again, there is nothing definitive in writing that ensures interventions are given.
UDL and Assistive Technology	The district does not have a firm understanding of how to incorporate Universal Designs for Learning. Teachers struggle making sure students have alternative ways of learning the content or showing what they know. Technology is used more for students with severe disabilities but mainly for Some students with more severe disabilities use assistive technology but it is not readily accessible for other students. It's not thought of as a strategy.
Social Emotional Learning (SEL)	Socioemotional learning is somewhat incorporated, but it's not embedded throughout the school or classroom. Very limited professional development on how to incorporate SEL into lessons.
Assessment used to inform instruction and tiered supports (how and why)	The assessment data is used to inform instruction for some students but not all. MAP has been the main district assessment used to track student progress. The BLT uses state assessment to identify building goals. Seems like a mismatch at best. Teachers create their own assessment to guide instruction not it's not really used at TBT meetings. There is an at-risk screening tool that is used to identify students who may need behavioral interventions and supports but it's not used consistently and the strategies are loosely monitored.

(Continued)

(Continued)	
Data Literacy	Teachers are *not* data literate. The instructional coaches are data literate. They will look at student data from MAP or DIBEL to make recommendations to the DLT and BLT. They are seen as keepers of the data rather than building the data literacy of the teachers.

This is a reflection of the Guiding Questions. The names and some details have been changed to protect confidentiality.

I was pretty surprised and shocked as I collected information for this part of the Equity Audit. As I reviewed my data, I came to two major conclusions. First, I realized our district doesn't officially set any type of academic expectations for students with disabilities. When I first thought about the question of, "Do we set high expectations for all students?" my immediate response was, "Yes, of course we set high expectations for all students." I realized that *I personally* set (what I think) are high expectations for my students, with little to no support or guidance from the special education department on what these high expectations should look like. The SPED administration also doesn't have a system in place to ensure students are having high expectations set for them.

If I wrote an IEP that set a lower (just more than trivial) standard for learning, I'm not sure my administrator would even notice. However, the student's parents could obviously argue that I failed to provide their child with a FAPE because the IEP was inadequate. Based on the *Endrew F.* standard, my district would probably fail to provide evidence that the IEP was reasonably calculated to ensure the student made a year's worth of progress.

The first leadership action I would take is a year of professional development to the special education staff. I'd communicate that the goals of every student's IEP need to be reasonably calculated to the student's skills and abilities, while also showing a year's worth of growth. The PD would include using mock IEPs to show how they would be inadequate in court (based on the higher *Endrew F.* standard*)*, and would provide specific feedback on why it was inadequate. As Hattie (Hattie & Zierer, 2017) explains in his book *10 Mindframes for Visible Learning: Teaching for Success,* professional development opportunities (which can have an effect size of 0.63), can help teachers gain a better understanding of the law and tasks they need to complete, and it could "provide them with concrete goals and steps for improving and evaluating their instruction" (2017, p. 30).

The second leadership action I would take is conducting internal audit of the special education department to evaluate the quality of IEPs.

My second conclusion from the audit was how data illiterate the staff at my school are. I was unaware this was such a problem at my school, and just assumed teachers were familiar with how data should be used to guide instruction. While all teachers in my school need to become data literate, I would start with the special education teachers because we have to do better by our students.

CONDITION FOUR: RESOURCES

Sample response to one of the guiding questions:
What could be structural antecedents of the causal data?

The results of adequately funding programs and personnel were contributed to the overall achievement of the school district. The data indicated a continuous climb in the state rankings over a three-year period of time. The district attributed the improved achievement because of the strategic use of district resources. However, the district stressed that increased student growth must still improve. Assessment results in English Language Arts showed academic growth while math scores declined.

The ELA results were for three consecutive years. So after the DLT analyzed the results, it was decided that an instructional coach would hire to focus on reading, writing, speaking, listing, and language. The district increased testing across subjects since those areas would also impact other subjects. By adding an effective ELA instructional coach the district improved student scores across all subjects but math remained stagnant.

CONDITION FIVE: GOVERNANCE

Sample response from a guiding question:
What does the data show?

The superintendent works alongside a set of board members that oversees the district.

The sponsor of a school must monitor and evaluate the academic and fiscal performance and the organization and operation of the community school on at least an annual basis. The special education law requires students to be educated in their least restrictive environment (LRE), yet our administrators lack the understanding of how to make informed decision based on what student needs versus what's more convenient for taking care of problems. Also, the number of students being disciplined, and removed, are not in line with Individual with Disabilities Education Act (IDEA) and Section 504 of the Americans with Disabilities Act (ADA) policies for providing access to education. Manifestation meetings are held but the procedures for ensuring new plans are being revised, updated, and followed are not being met.

APPENDIX E: DOUBLE HELIX SYSTEM OF SUPPORT

CLARITY

A strength-based system of support is the foundation for the broader school improvement process by supporting all learners and for ensuring equitable access to a high-quality education.

- A nimble and responsive system is defined for growth, support, and achievement
- High expectations by the adults are evident
- Accountability is measured by evidence of impact

DESIGN FEATURES

The tiers are banned and replaced with effective instruction, intervention, and acceleration practices delivered with precision and in real time.

- Staff are comprehensively situated inside the classroom
- Nimble and responsive strategies are delivered with precision
- Interventions are identified not students
- Data is used to inform, monitor, and adjust
- Indicators are used to monitor growth

SHARED ACCOUNTABILITY

Shared accountability is non-negotiable.

- Interdependencies are anchored to the improvement process
- Adult competencies are strategically supported
- Academic and social dimensions of learning are delivered with precision
- A collaborative team structure is deeply implemented and is responsible for all students

APPENDIX F: DOUBLE HELIX SYSTEM OF SUPPORT DESCRIPTION

Each strand of the Double Helix serves as the complementary backbone of the other, creating a complete structure. The elements are nondirectional, and yet absolutely dependent upon the whole, creating a cohesive system. In other words, when we get the conditions right—everyone in the system wins. Students along the full continuum of learning, can engage with ambitious content, supported by real-time differentiated instruction, and teachers using the right data to make actionable adjustments so students grow.

The elements of a comprehensive Double Helix System of Support that are designed to achieve this comprehensive approach include the following:

A Clear Definition: A nimble and responsive System of Support (SoS) which encompasses the academic and social dimensions of learning serves as the overarching frame. It provides the foundation for the broader school improvement process by supporting all learners and ensures equitable access to high-quality education.

Shared Accountability: Implementation is the collective responsibility of all educators, staff, families, and communities. The adult skills needed for meeting the full continuum of learners is provided by, supported, and monitored by district and school leadership teams. That means a productive collaborative team structure whereby all educators are comprehensively situated for the maximum benefit of all students.

Design: High expectations of the adults working with students is nonnegotiable. A nimble design enables educators to make data-informed decisions that meet the needs of students from different backgrounds, levels of language proficiency, learning complexities, and levels of attainment. Strategies that address needs are identified and intentionally designed. Academic and behavioral instruction and support is implemented with stretch inside the classroom. The tiers formerly used to label students would be banned.

There are high expectations for the educational, financial, and human resources that will be intentionally allocated and coordinated across and within the system and in every classroom. A strength-based approach that meets the needs of students, including those with complex needs and disabilities, will be designed, implemented, and monitored for effectiveness.

REFERENCES

Allen, L. (2001, December). From plaques to practice: How schools can breathe life into their guiding beliefs. *Phi Delta Kappan, 83*(4), 289–293.

Board of Ed. of Hendrick Hudson Central School Dist., Westchester Cty. v. Rowley, 458 U.S. 176, 102 S.Ct. 3034, 73 L.Ed.2d 690. 458 U.S. 176 (1982). https://supreme.justia.com/cases/federal/us/458/176/

Calgary Board of Education. (2023, February). *Mathematics: Use & connect mathematical representations.* https://www.cbe.ab.ca/about-us/policies-and-regulations/Documents/Mathematics-Use-and-Connect-Multiple-Representations.pdf

Center on Reinventing Public Education. (2022). *The state of the American student: Fall 2022.* https://crpeorg.wpengine.com/wp-content/uploads/CRPE-%E2%80%94-Profile-of-a-Student-Report.pdf

Center on the Developing Child. (n.d.). *What is executive function? And how does it relate to child development?* https://developingchild.harvard.edu/resources/what-is-executive-function-and-how-does-it-relate-to-child-development/#:~:text=The%20phrase%20%E2%80%9Cexecutive%20function%E2%80%9D%20refers,focused%20despite%20distractions%2C%20among%20others

Connecticut State Department of Education, Bureau of Special Education. (2022). *New IEP/CT-SEDS.* https://portal.ct.gov/SDE/Special-Education/New-IEP/New-IEP-CT-SEDS

DuFour, R., & Reeves, D. (2016, March 1). *The futility of PLC Lite.* https://kappanonline.org/the-futility-of-plc-lite/

Education for All Handicapped Children Act of 1975, Public Law 142, U.S. Statutes at Large 89 (1975), 773–796. https://www.govinfo.gov/content/pkg/STATUTE-89/pdf/STATUTE-89-Pg773.pdf

Endrew F. v. Douglas Co. School Dist. Re-1, 137 (2017). https://www.supremecourt.gov/opinions/16pdf/15-827_0pm1.pdf

Every Student Succeeds Act (ESSA), Public Law 114-95 (2015). https://www.govinfo.gov/content/pkg/PLAW-114publ95/pdf/PLAW-114publ95.pdf

Gershenson, S. (2022, November 2). *The power of expectations in district and charter schools.* The Thomas B. Fordham Institute. https://fordhaminstitute.org/national/research/the-power-of-expectations-district-charter

Grissom, J. A., Egalite, A. J., & Lindsay, C. A. (2021). *How principals affect students and schools: A systematic synthesis of two decades of research.* The Wallace Foundation. http://www.wallacefoundation.org/principalsynthesis

Hattie, J. (2023). *Visible learning: The sequel a synthesis of over 2,100 meta-analyses relating to achievement.* Routledge.

Hattie, J., Masters, D., & Birch, K. (2016). *Visible Learning into action: International case studies of impact.* Routledge.

Hattie, J., & Zierer, K. (2017). *10 mindframes for visible Learning: Teaching for success*. Routledge.

Hillis, S., N'konzi, J. N., Msemburi, W., Cluver, L., Villaveces, A., Flaxman, S., & Unwin, H. J. T. (2022). Orphanhood and caregiver loss among children based on new global excess COVID-19 death estimates. *JAMA Pediatrics, 176*(11), 1145–1148. https://doi.org10.1001/jamapediatrics.2022.3157

Ibarra, H., & Scoular, A. (2019, November 4). The leader as coach: How to unleash innovation, energy and commitment. *Harvard Business Review*. https://hbr.org/2019/11/the-leader-as-coach

Individuals with Disabilities Education Act, Public Law 94-142 (2004). https://www.govinfo.gov/content/pkg/STATUTE-89/pdf/STATUTE-89-Pg773.pdf

Jung, C. (2023, March 24). *Special education planning form gets revamp in Mass. for first time in 20 years*. WBUR. https://www.wbur.org/news/2023/03/24/special-education-improved-forms-process

Killian, S. (2015). *Eight strategies Robert Marzano & John Hattie agree on*. https://vtss-ric.vcu.edu/media/vtss-ric/documents/s2s-strand-2/2021-2022-session-a-non-accessible/session-b-accessible/quality-core-instructions/VCU-3396_02aag_8StrategiesRobertMarzanoandJohnHattieAgreeOnR1V2.pdf

Leithwood, K., Seashore, K., Anderson, S., Wahlstrom, K., & Center for Applied Research and Educational Improvement. (2004). *Review of research: How Leadership influences student learning*. University of Minnesota, Center for Applied Research and Educational Improvement.

Mahnken, K. (2023, June 21). *NAEP scores "flashing red" after a lost generation of learning for 13-year-olds*. The 74. https://www.the74million.org/article/naep-scores-flashing-red-after-a-lost-generation-of-learning-for-13-year-olds/#:~:text=Wednesday's%20publication%20of%20scores%20from,in%20the%201990s%3B%20struggling%20readers

National Assessment of Educational Progress. (2023). *NAEP long-term trend assessment results: Reading and mathematics: Reading and mathematics scores decline during COVID-19 pandemic*. https://www.nationsreportcard.gov/highlights/ltt/2022/

National Center for Education Statistics. (2022, July 6). *More than 80 percent of U.S. public schools report pandemic has negatively impacted student behavior and socio-emotional development*. https://nces.ed.gov/whatsnew/press_releases/07_06_2022.asp

Office of Special Education Programs. (2021, May 26). *OSEP fast facts: School aged children 5 (in kindergarten) through 21 served under Part B, of the IDEA*. https://sites.ed.gov/idea/osep-fast-facts-school-aged-children-5-21-served-under-idea-part-b-21/

Owen, K. K. (n.d.). *A six-step process to improvement that school districts can replicate. Studer Education*. https://www.studereducation.com/six-step-improvement-process-for-school-districts/

Parsonson, B. S. (2012). Evidence-based classroom behaviour management strategies. *Kairaranga, 13*(1), 16–23. https://files.eric.ed.gov/fulltext/EJ976654.pdf

Reeves, D. (2019). *Achieving equity and excellence: Immediate results from the lessons of high-poverty, high-success schools (A strategy guide to equitable classroom practices and results for high-poverty schools)*. Solution Tree Press.

Reeves, D. (2020). *FAST feedback: Keys to improved teaching and learning* [Video]. YouTube. https://www.creativeleadership.net/resources-content/fast-feedback-keys-to-improved-teaching-and-learning

REFERENCES

Reeves, D. (2023). *Fearless coaching: Resilience and results from the classroom to the boardroom.* Archway.

Roza, M., & Silberstein, K. (2023, June 15). *Districts now have more staff than ever. And fewer students. What happens next?* https://edunomicslab.org/wp-content/uploads/2023/06/30-min-webinar_staff-v-enroll_final.pdf

Siang, S., & Canning, M. (2023, February 23). Coaching your team as a collective makes it stronger. *Harvard Business Review.* https://hbr.org/2023/02/coaching-your-team-as-a-collective-makes-it-stronger

Sugai, G. (2010). Realizing the potential of RTI—How comprehensive is implementation? *NCLD's RTI Leadership Forum.* https://www.youtube.com/watch?v=XEev_E7MLF4

Trach, S. (2014). Inspired instructional coaching: Stimulate teaching by structuring meaningful observations and feedback that will improve instruction schoolwide. *Principal,* (November/December), pp. 13–16. https://www.naesp.org/sites/default/files/Trach_ND14.pdf

Zirkel, P. A. (n.d.). *Implementation of response to intervention (RTI) and multi-tiered systems of support (MTSS).*

INDEX

A Sage Company

Helping educators make the greatest impact

CORWIN HAS ONE MISSION: to enhance education through intentional professional learning.

We build long-term relationships with our authors, educators, clients, and associations who partner with us to develop and continuously improve the best evidence-based practices that establish and support lifelong learning.

Keep Learning...

The
Education
Policy &
Practice
Group

The Education Policy & Practice Group offers future-focused, equity-based consulting that leads to improved academic and social-emotional outcomes for students. We help institutions and agencies develop efficient, fair funding models, innovative policy, and improved organizations.

We Empower
by providing senior leadership the tools to design and maintain equitable and ambitious systems, including public-private partnerships, industry best practices and growth mindsets.

We Partner
with every type of organization—including federal, state, and local agencies as well as education and nonprofit organizations at every level—to build sustainable pathways for effective and efficient operations and practices.

We Collaborate
with institutes of higher education, aligning policies and practices to ensure high quality preparation programs for teachers. We understand that when teachers are supported professionally, they are better equipped to ensure success for more students.

It's common for organizations and institutions to take a top-down approach to policy reform. But significant research clearly demonstrates that **for policy to drive change, change needs to happen from the inside out**. Both need to work together in tandem to reach a common solution in the middle. Practice should inform policy and policy should back up the practice.

To learn more, visit **edpolicyconsulting.com**